Language Arts
Workbook A

Siegfried Engelmann

Jean Osborn

Karen Davis

Evan Haney

Owen Engelmann

Acknowledgments

The authors are grateful to the following people for their assistance in the preparations of Reading Mastery Transformations Grade K Language.

Cally Dwyer
Katherine Gries
Debbi Kleppen
Patricia McFadden
Melissa Morrow

mheducation.com/prek-12

Copyright © 2021 McGraw-Hill Education

All rights reserved. No part of this publication may be reproduced or distributed in any form or by any means, or stored in a database or retrieval system, without the prior written consent of McGraw-Hill Education, including, but not limited to, network storage or transmission, or broadcast for distance learning.

Send all inquiries to:
McGraw-Hill Education
8787 Orion Place
Columbus, OH 43240

ISBN: 978-0-07-905552-1
MHID: 0-07-905552-4

Printed in the United States of America.

2 3 4 5 6 7 8 9 10 LMN 26 25 24 23 22 21

2

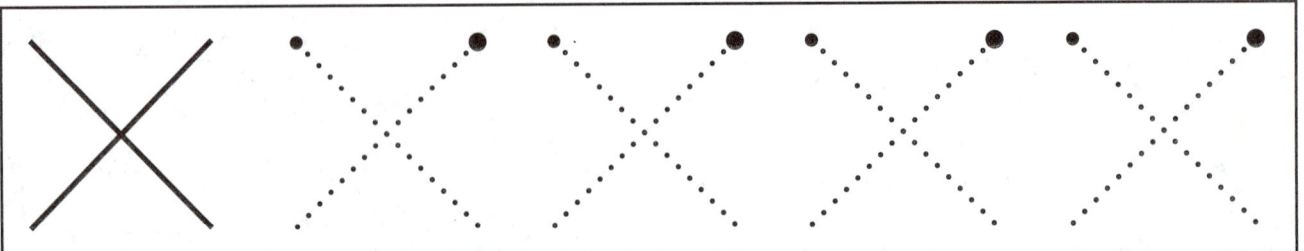

4

6

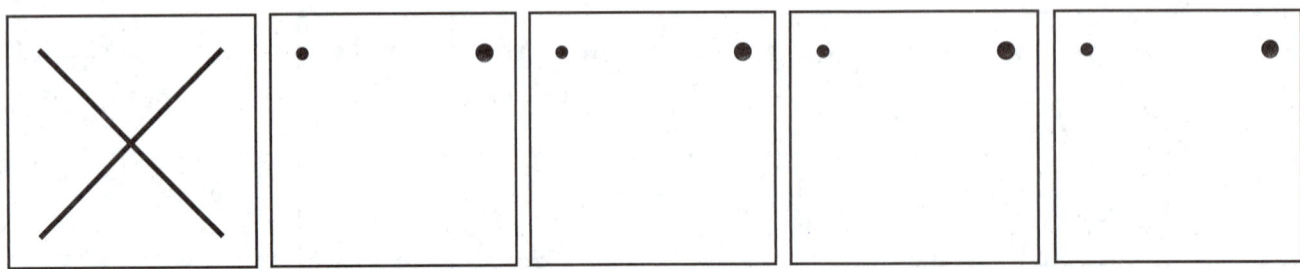

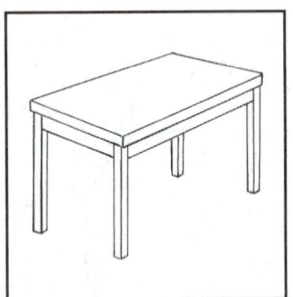 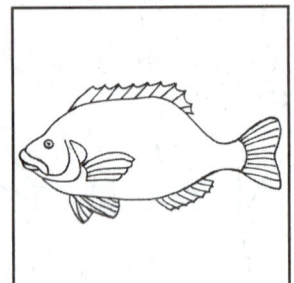 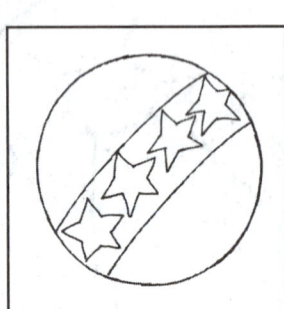 

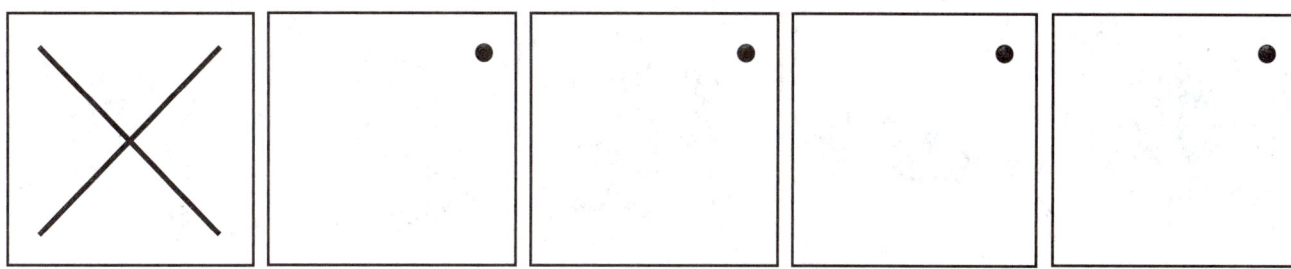

  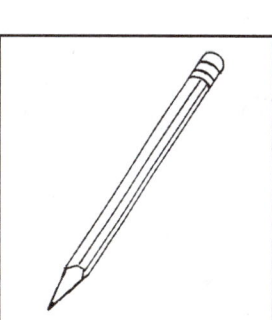 

 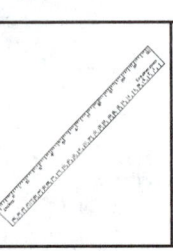     

 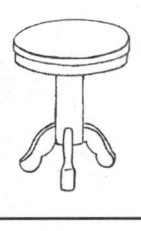    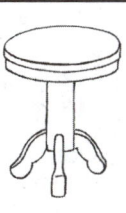 

10

  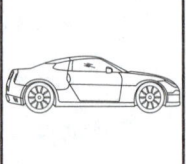    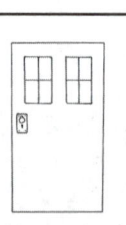

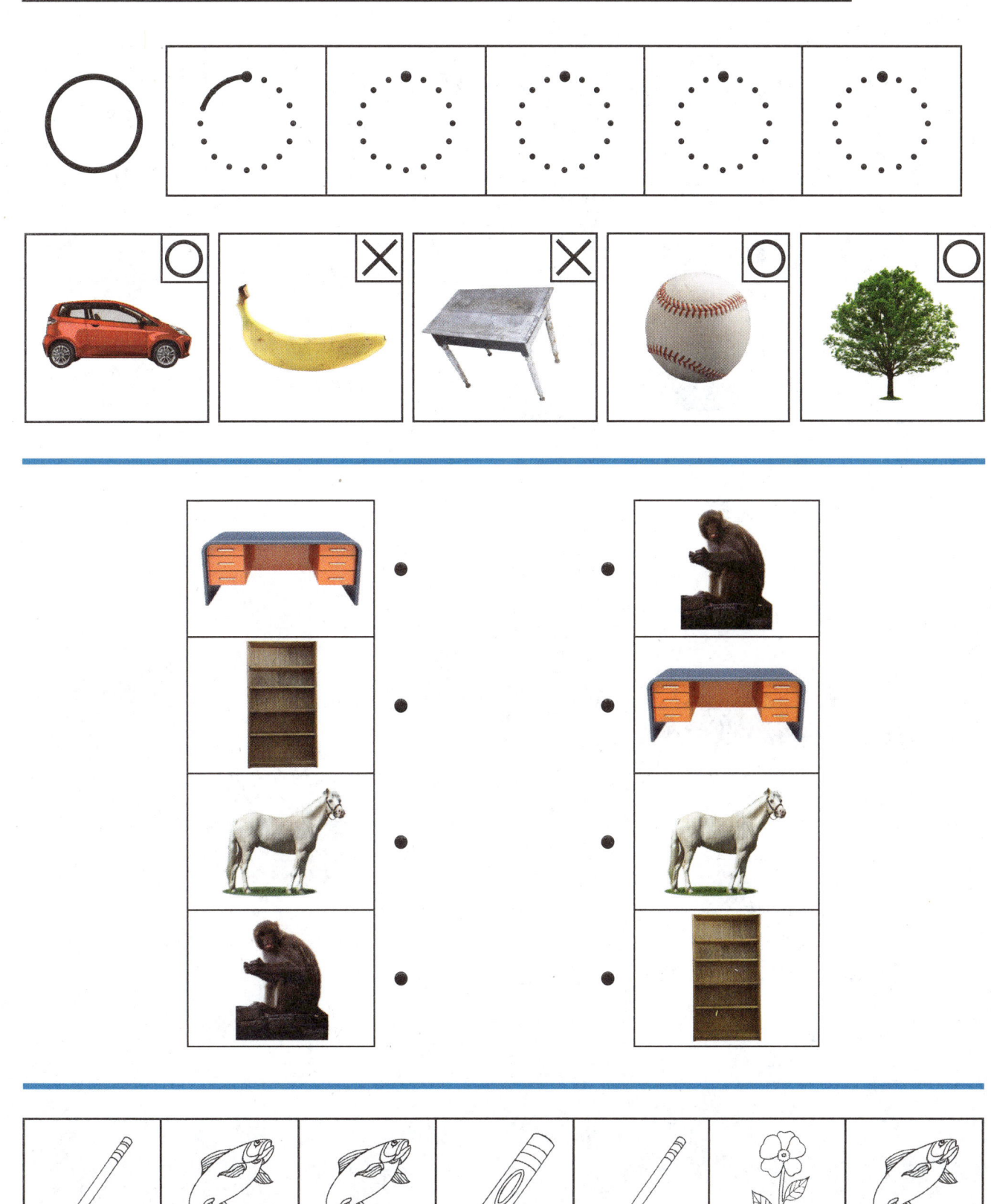

12

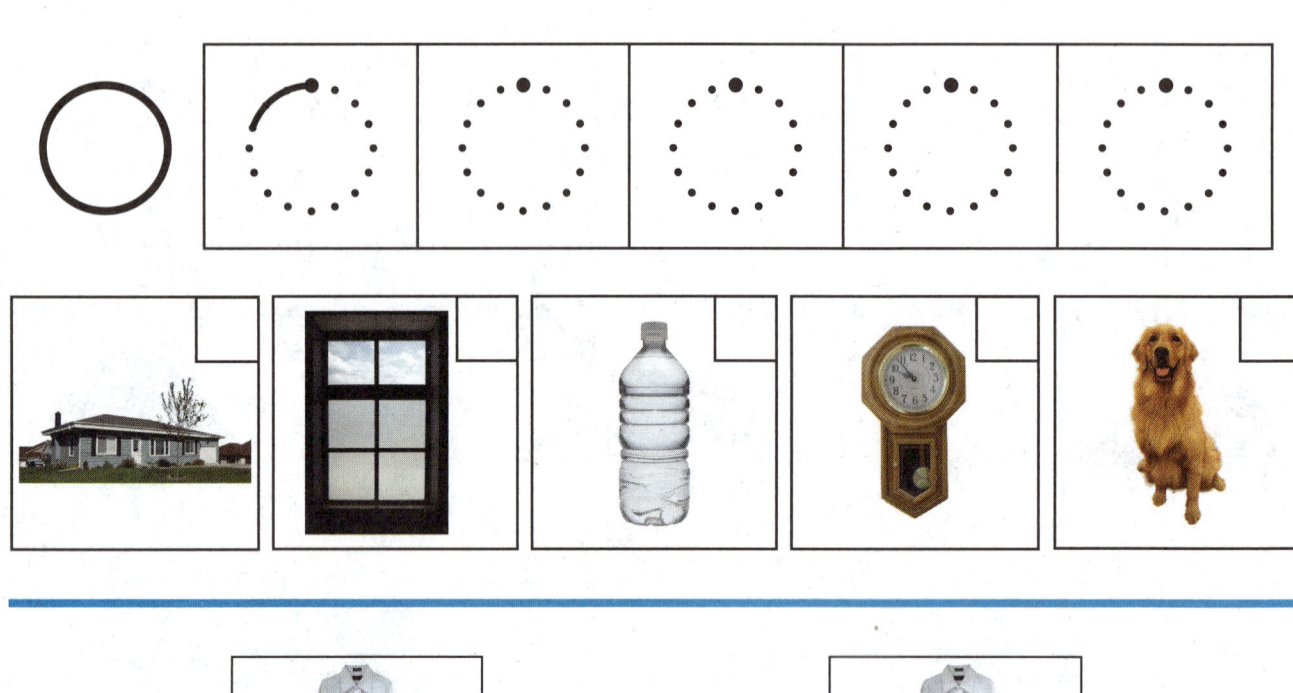

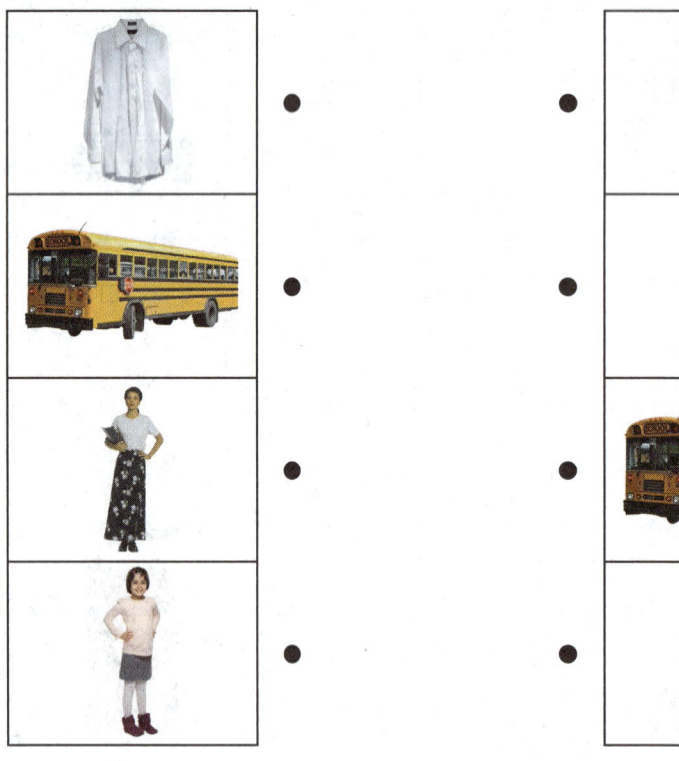

13

  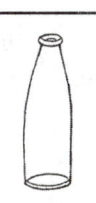    

14

    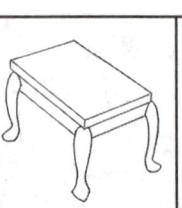  

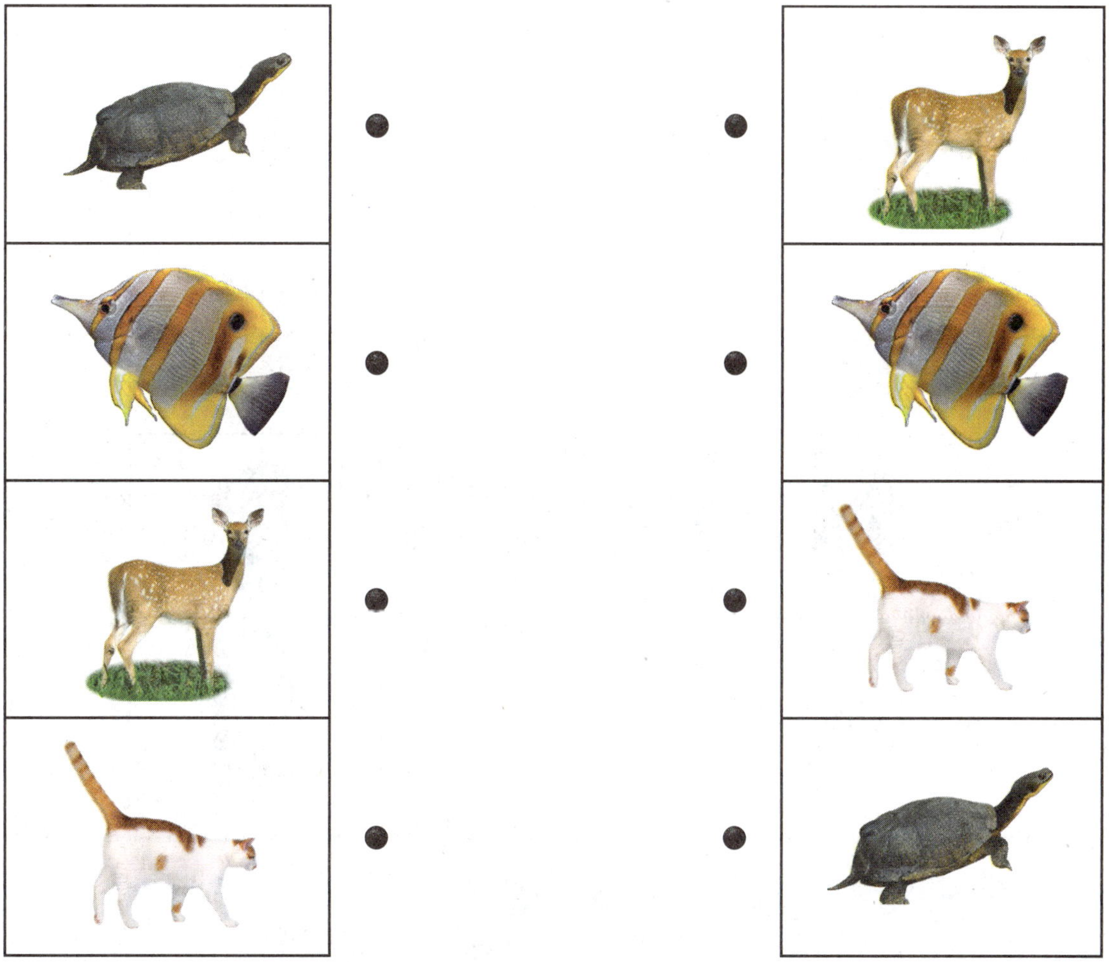

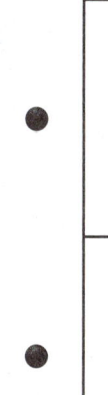

16

17

18

19

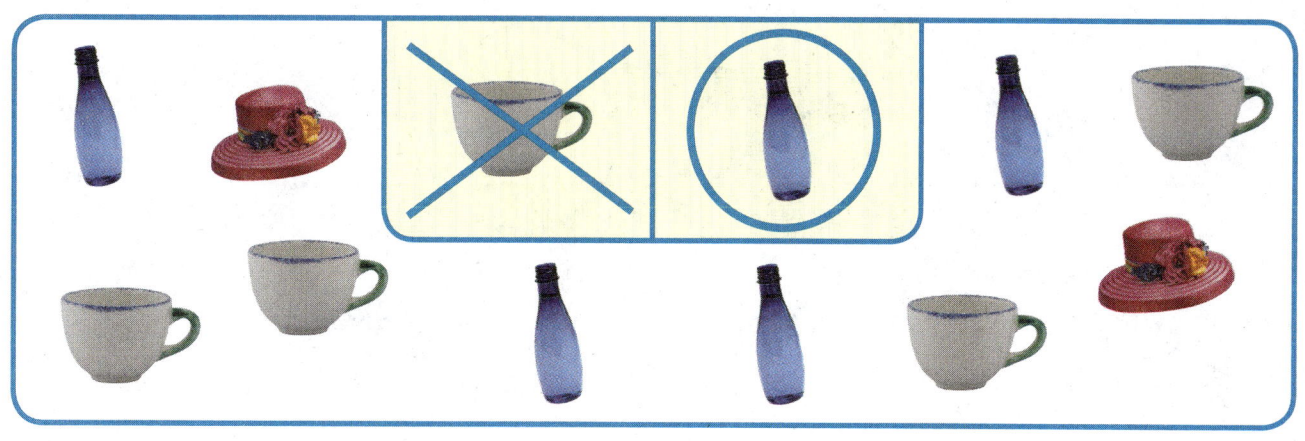

20

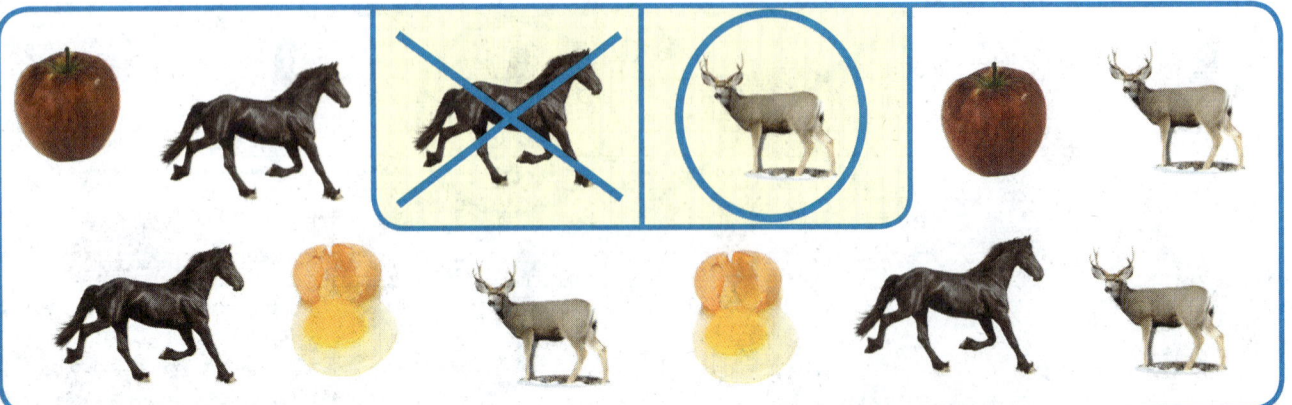

21

22

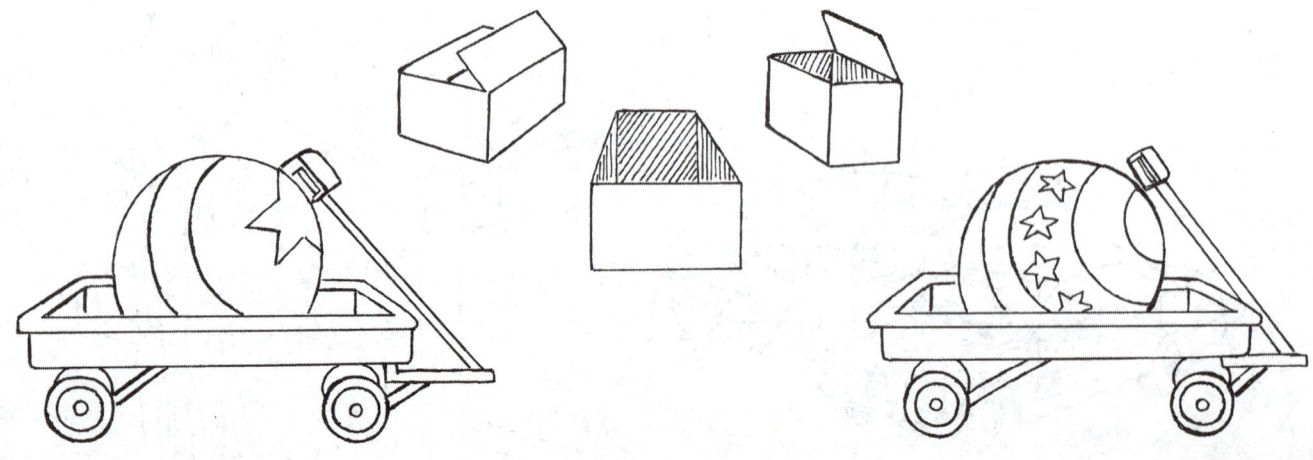

23

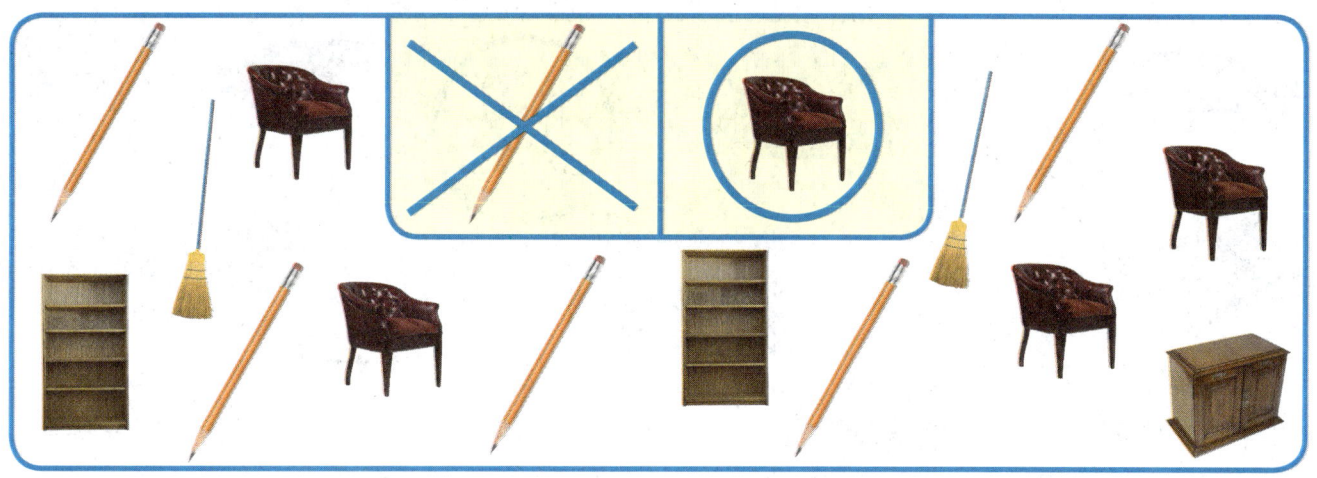

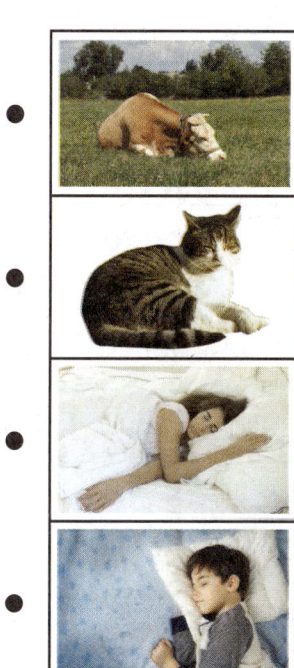

24

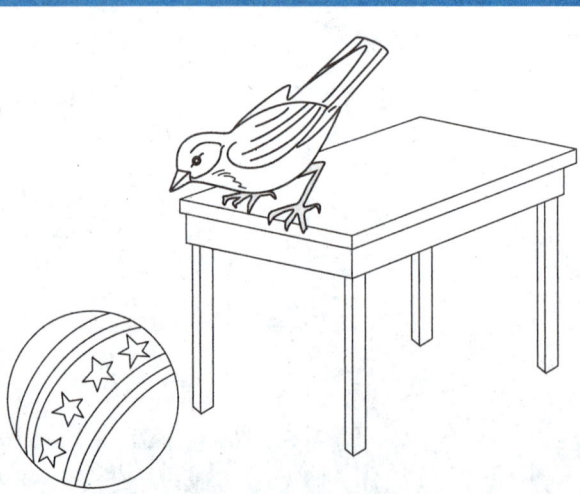

25

Side 1

Side 2

27

Side 1

Side 2

28

Side 1

Side 2

29

Side 1

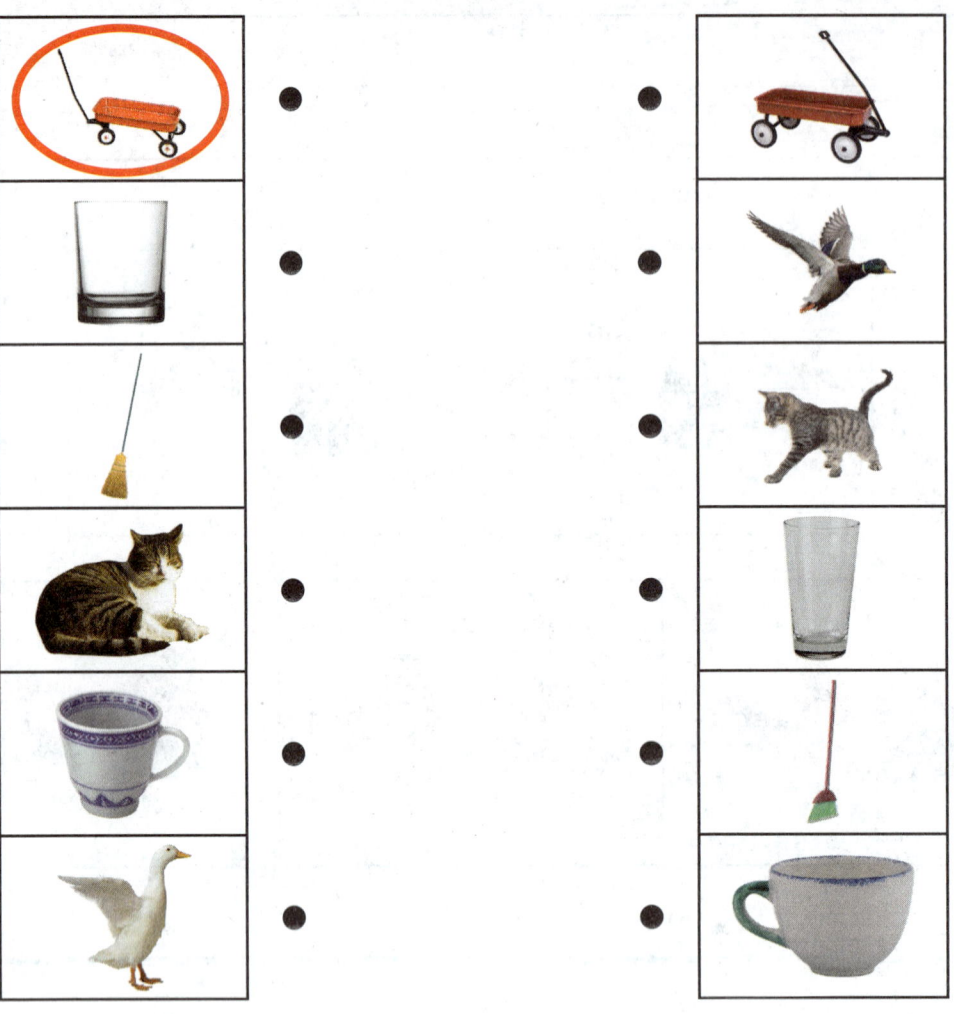

Side 2

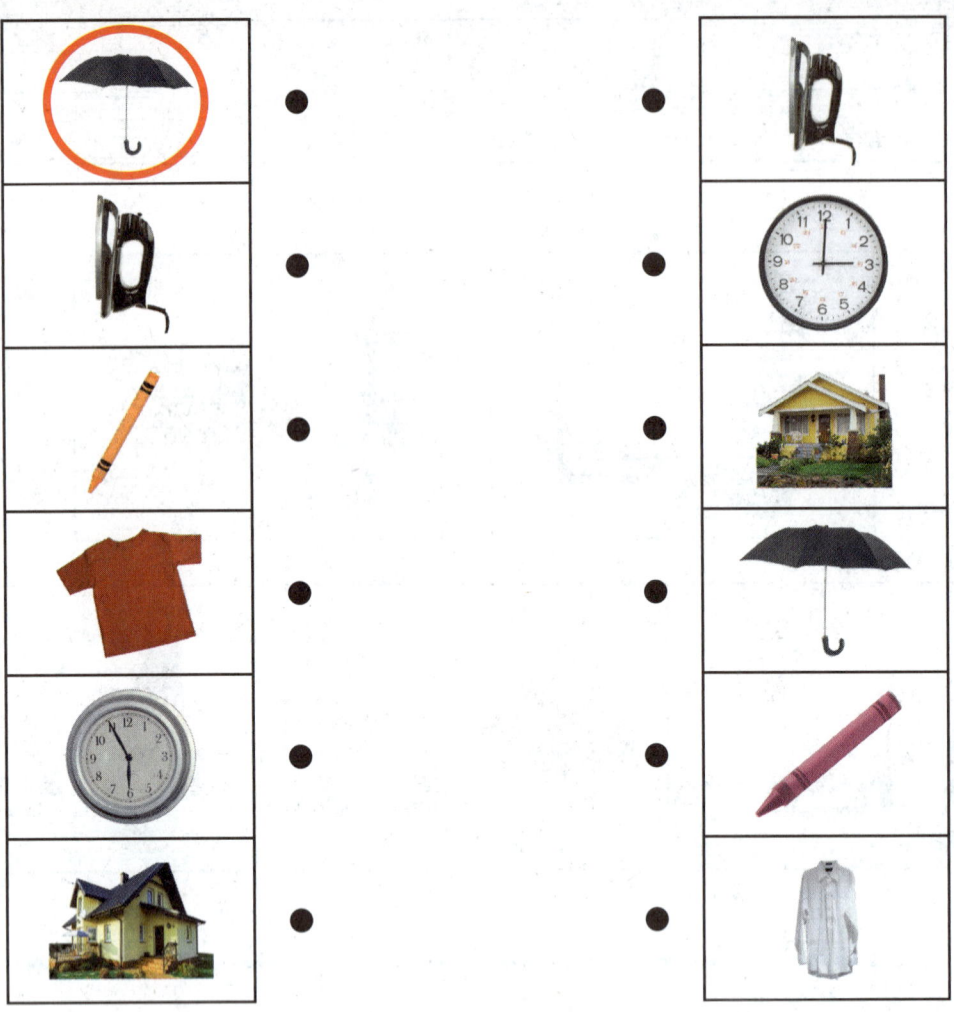

Side 2

31

Side 1

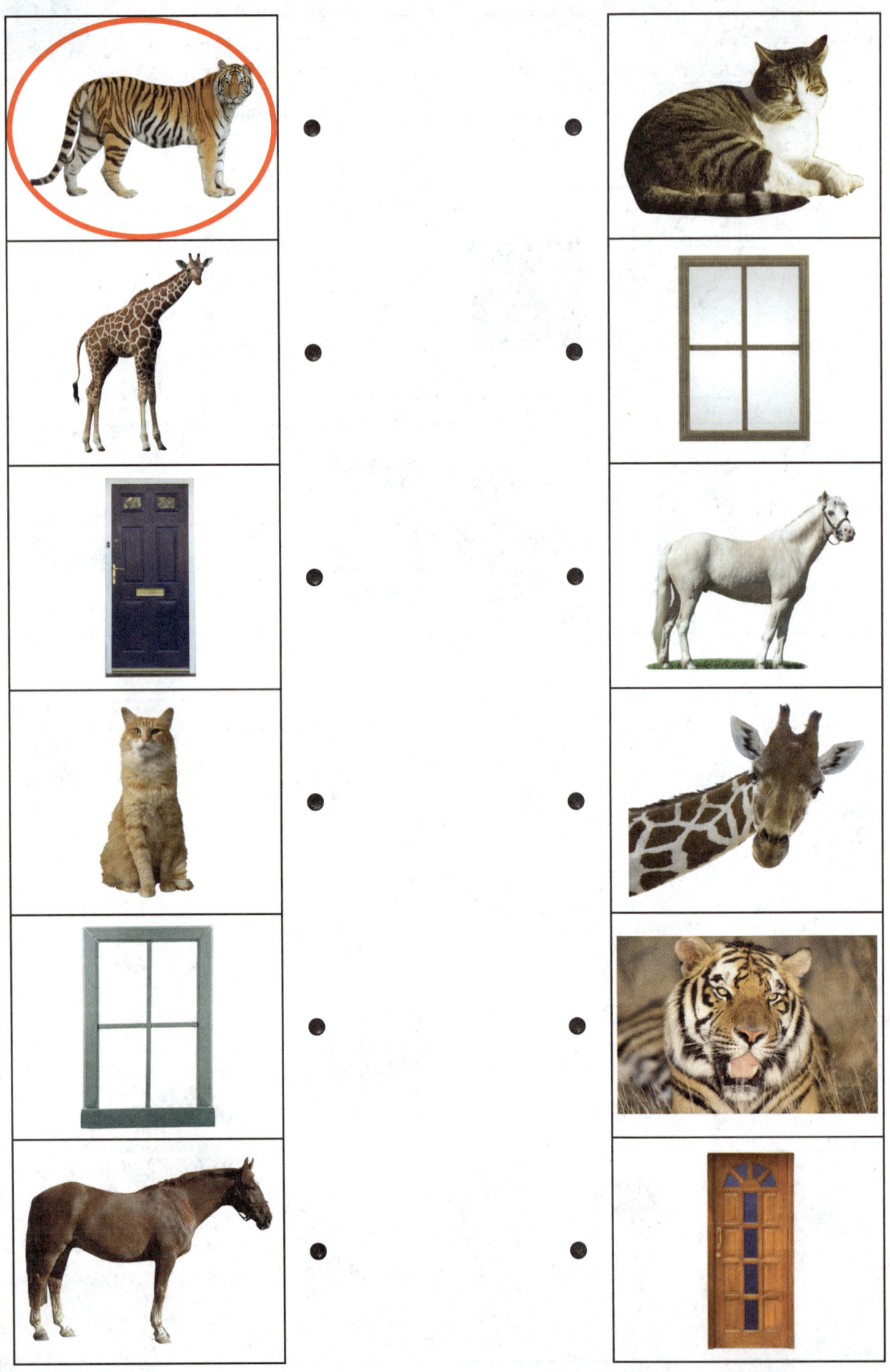

32

Side 1

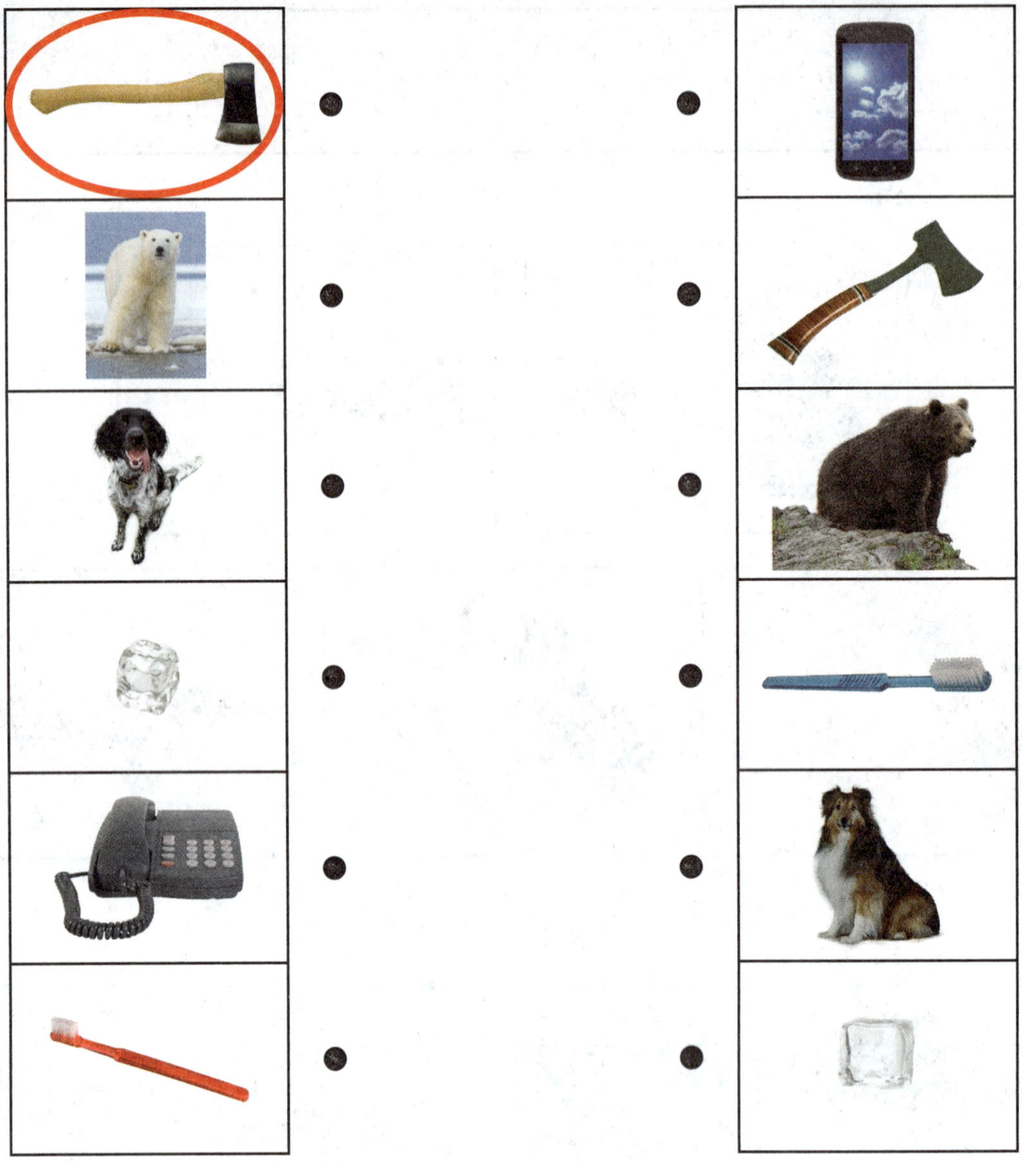

Side 2

33

Side 1

Side 2

34

Side 1

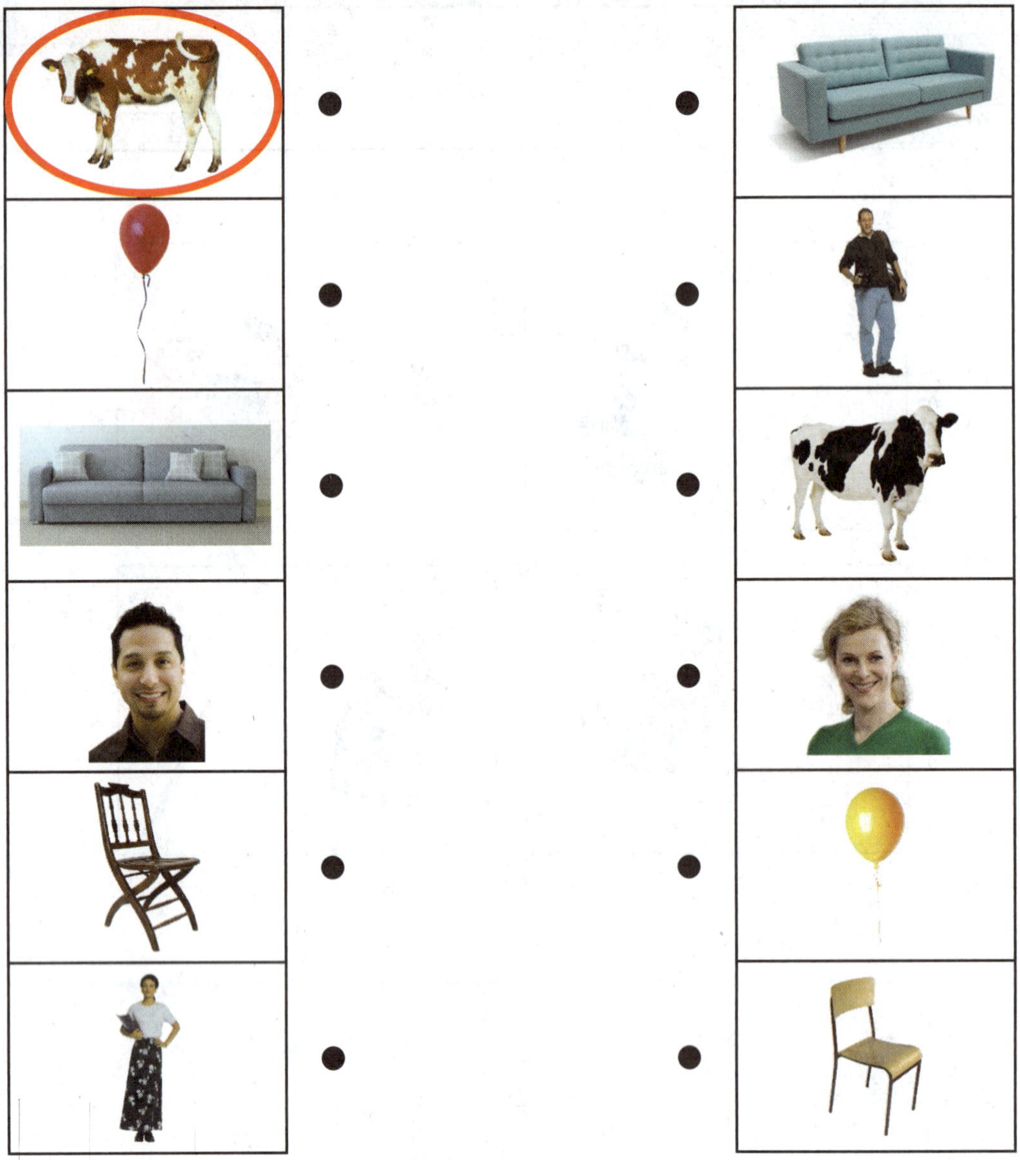

Side 2

35

Side 1

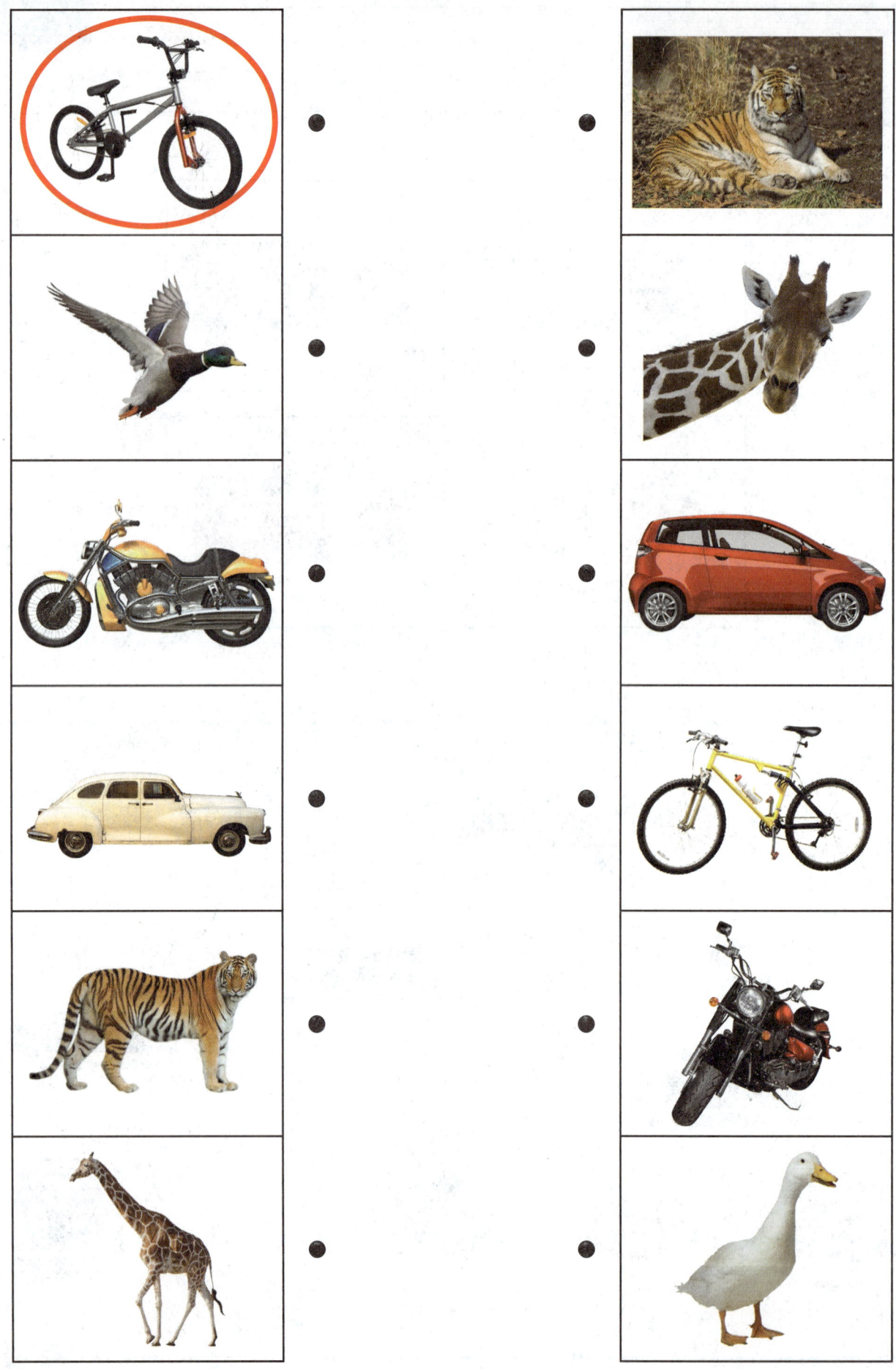

Side 2

36

Side 1

37

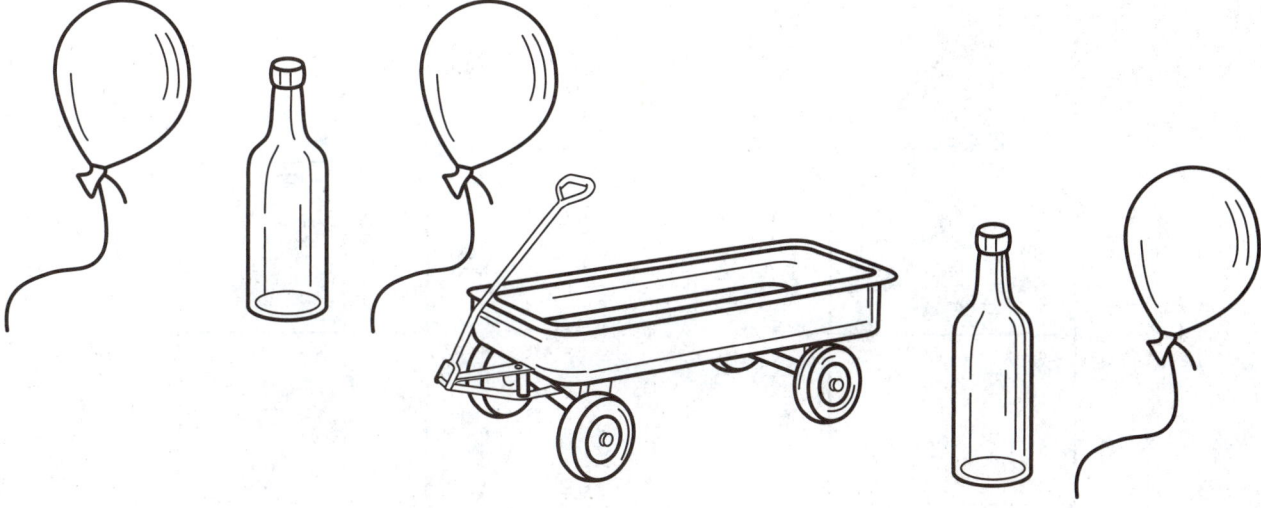

Side 1

Side 2

38

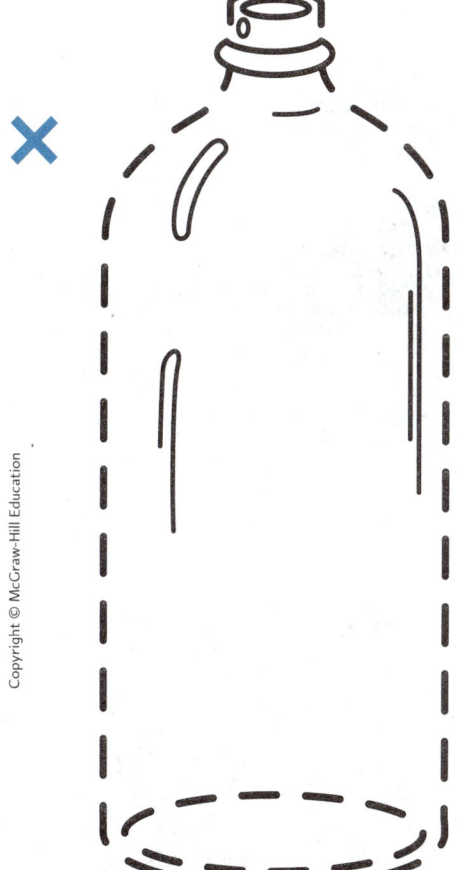

Side 1

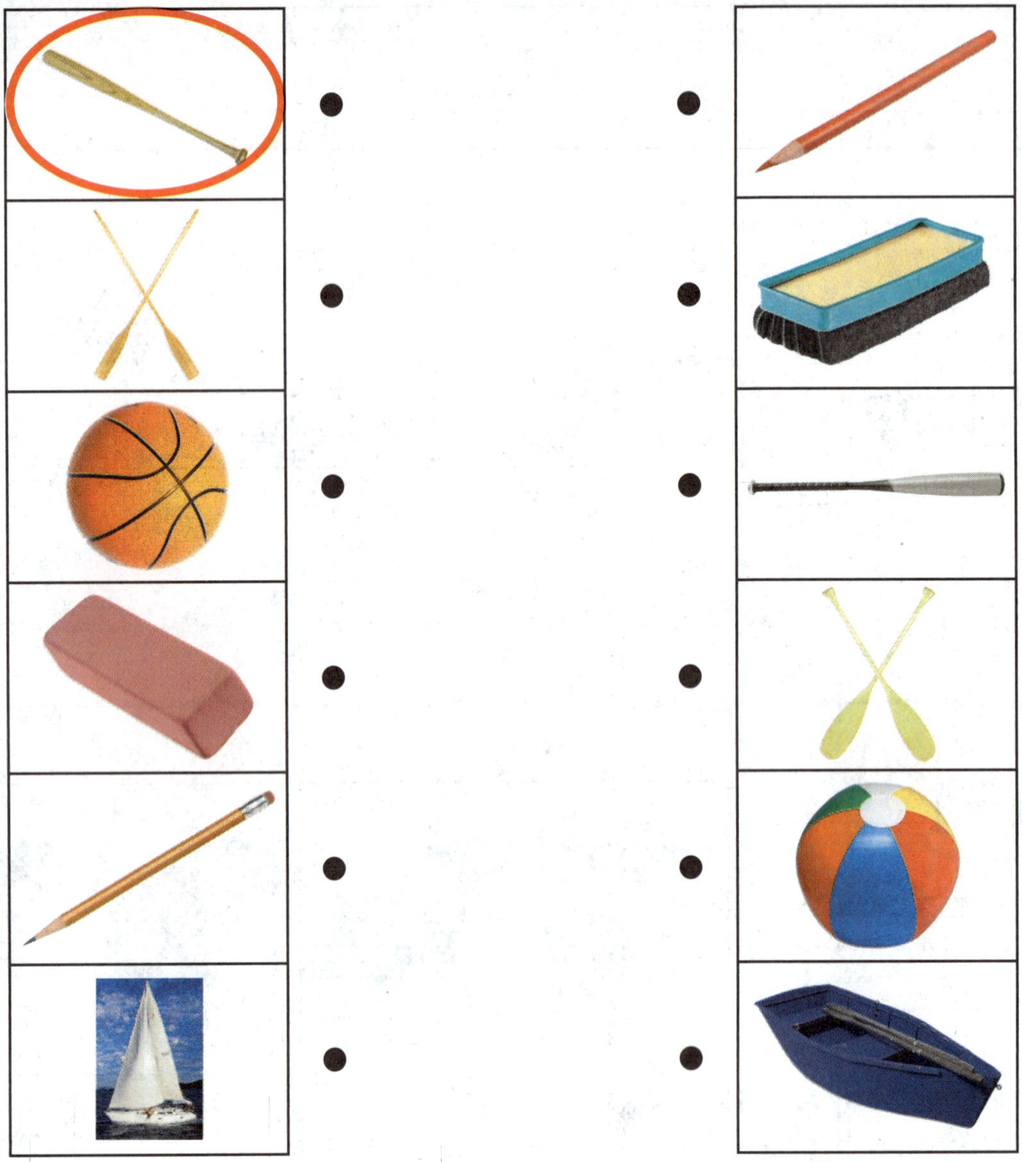

Side 2

39

Side 1

Side 2

40

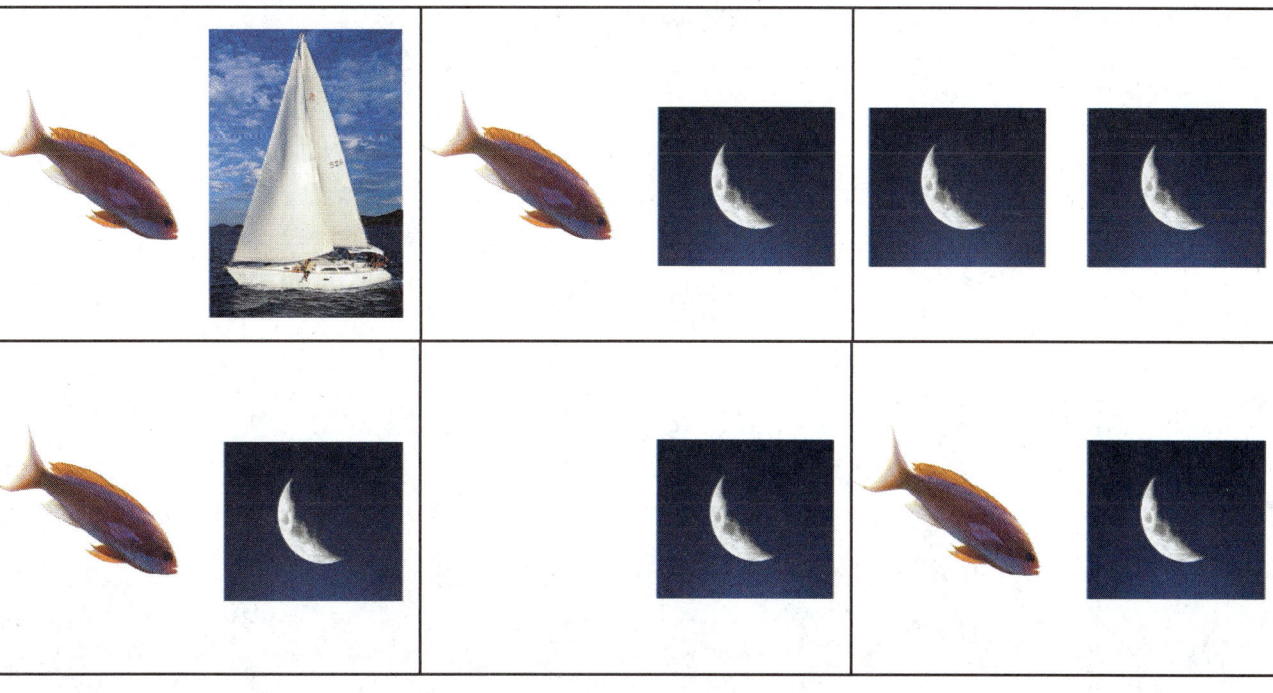

Side 1

Side 2

41

Side 1

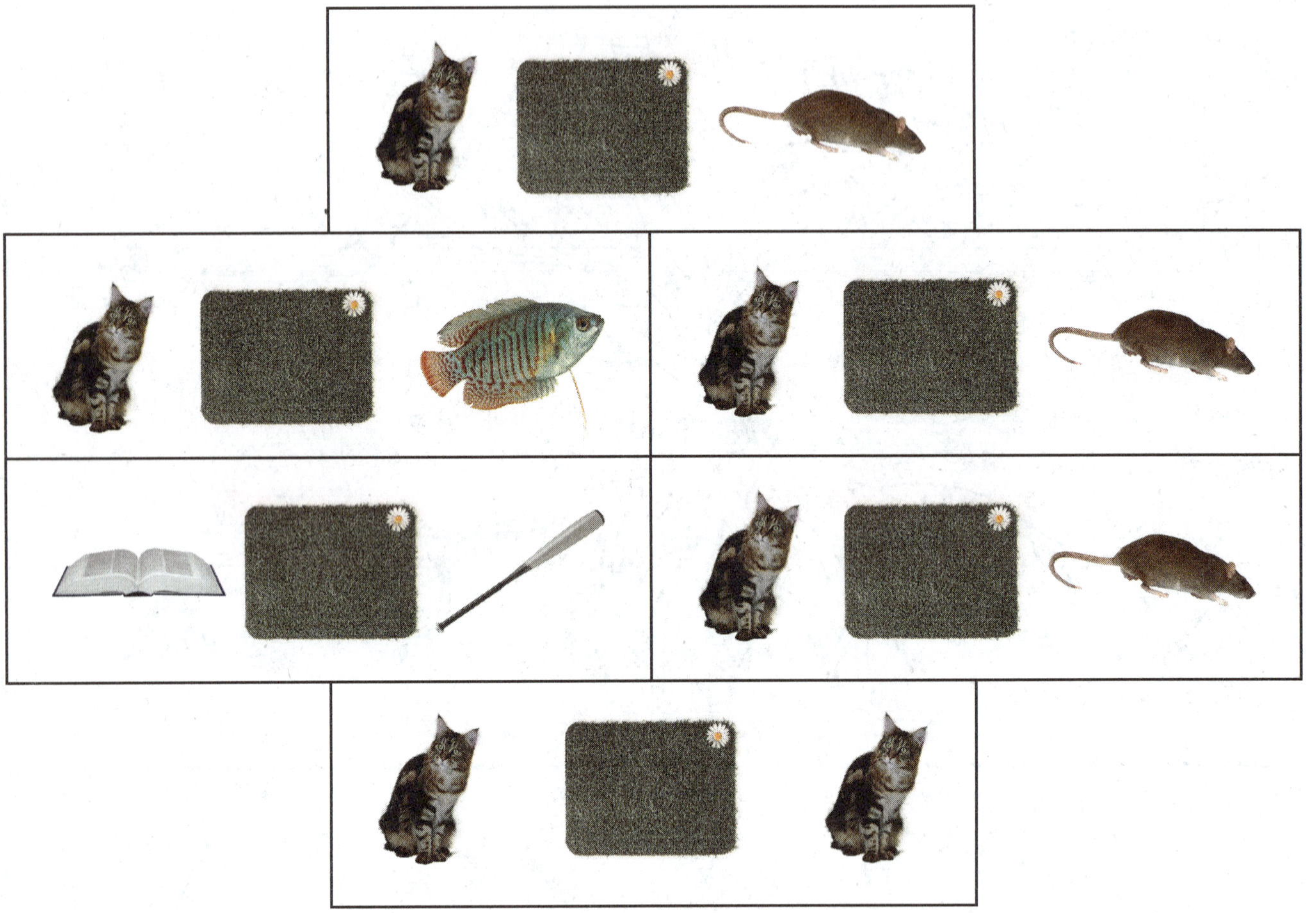

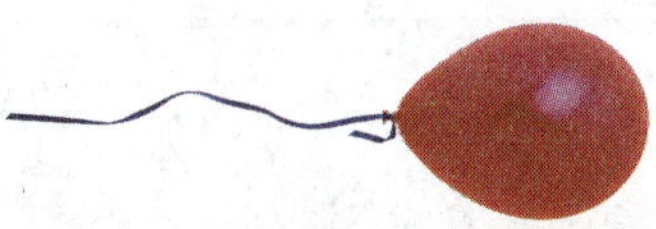

Side 2

42

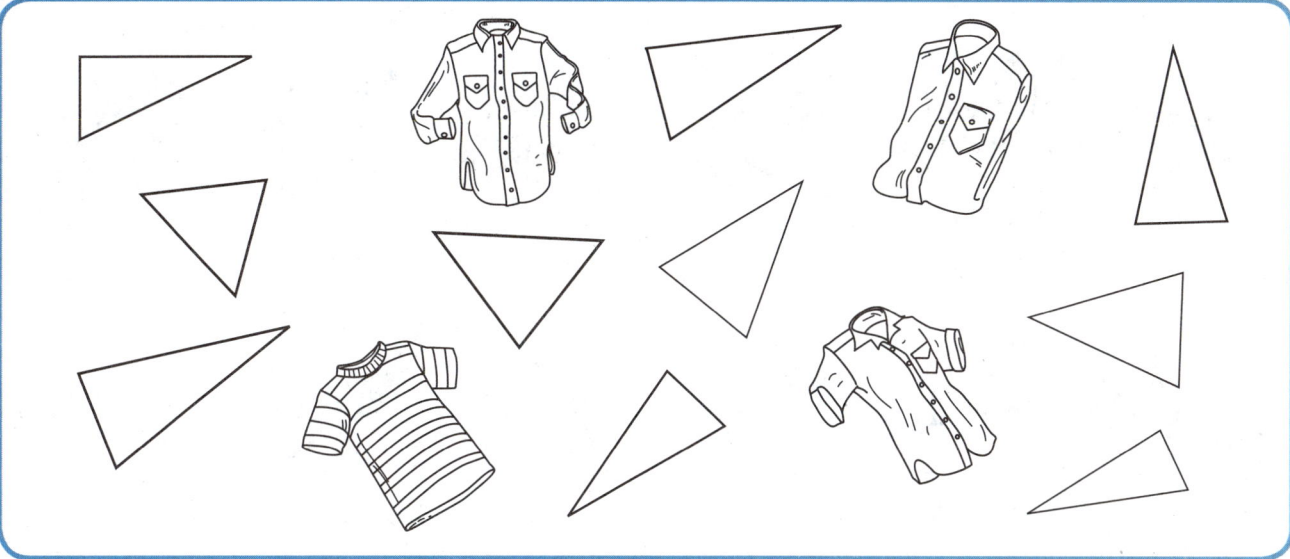

Side 1

Side 2

43

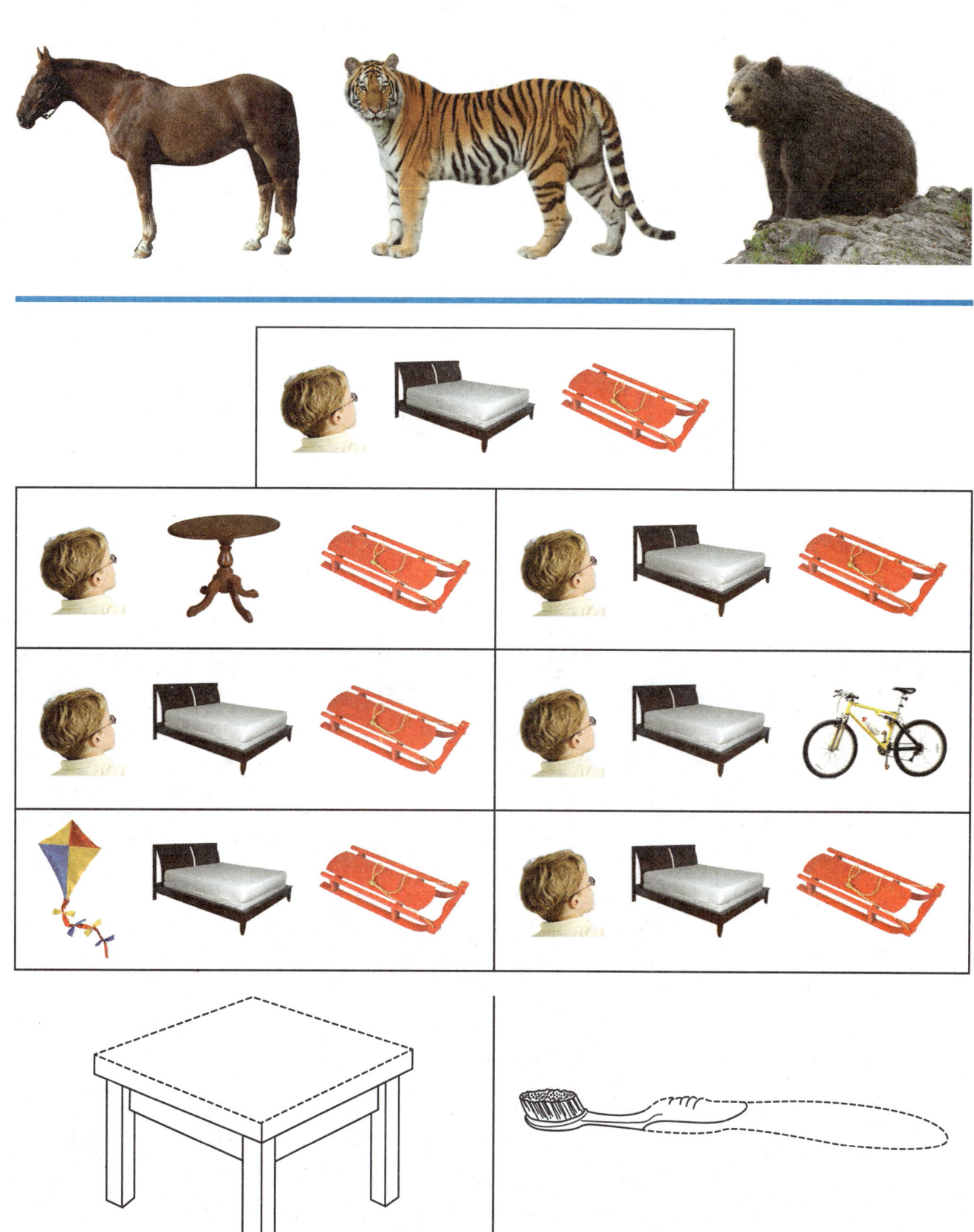

Side 1

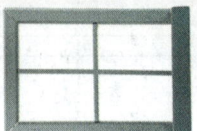

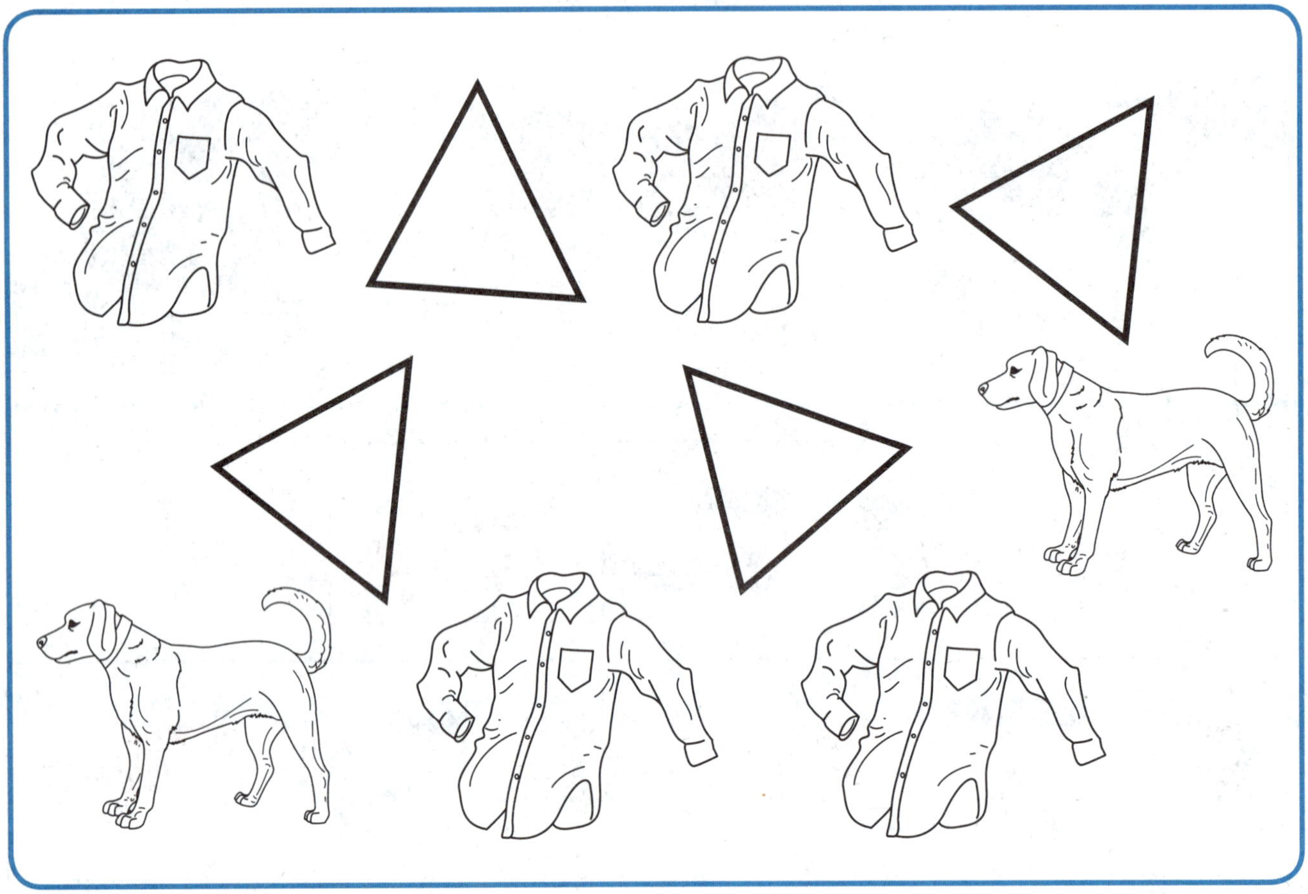

Side 2

44

Side 1

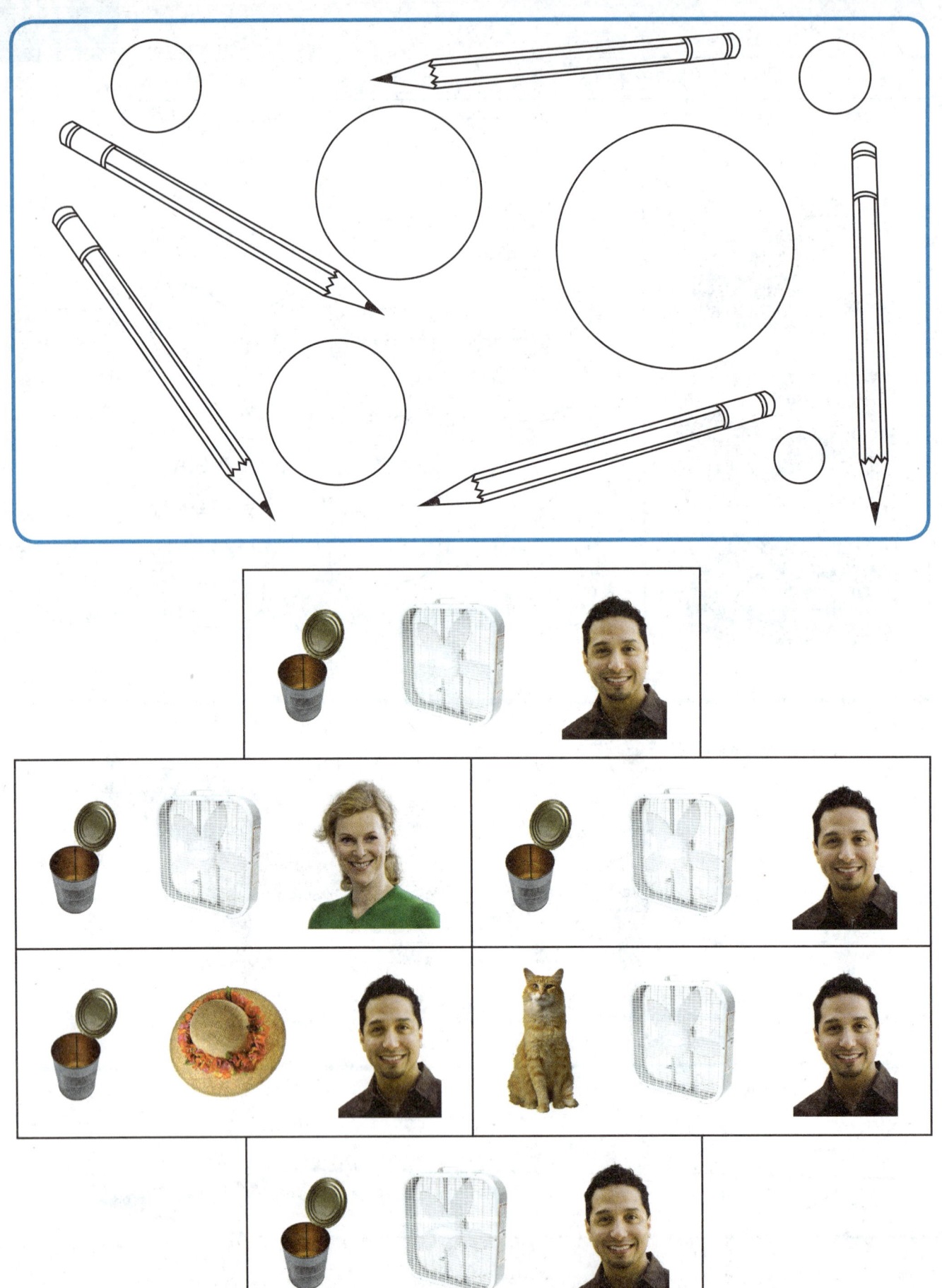

Side 2

45

Side 1

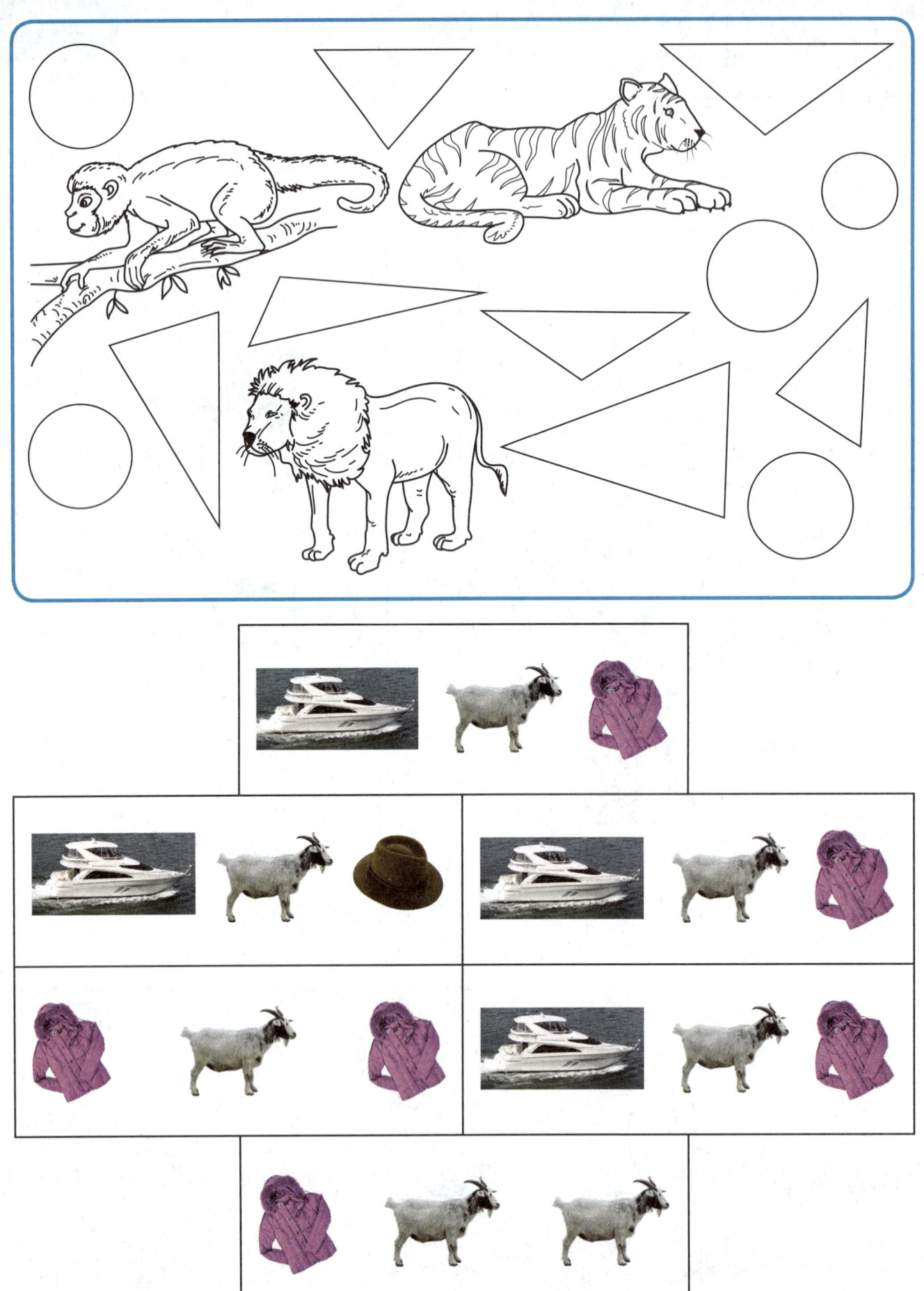

Side 2

46

Side 1

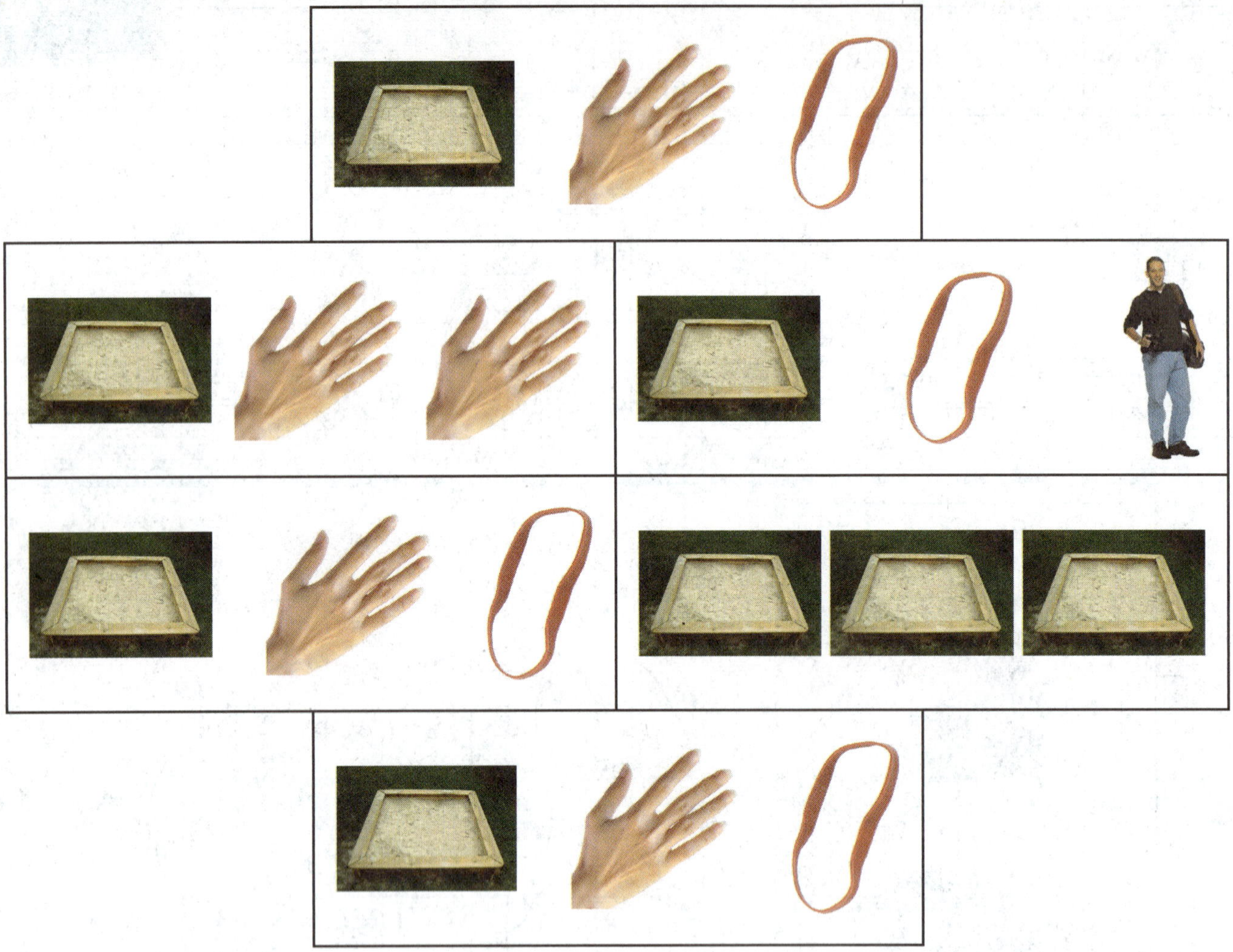

Side 2

47

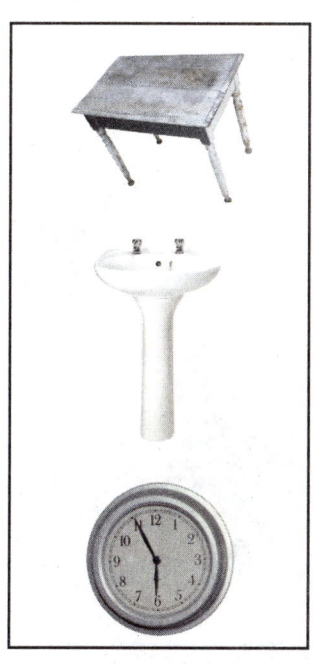 

Side 1

Side 2

48

Side 1

Side 2

49

Side 1

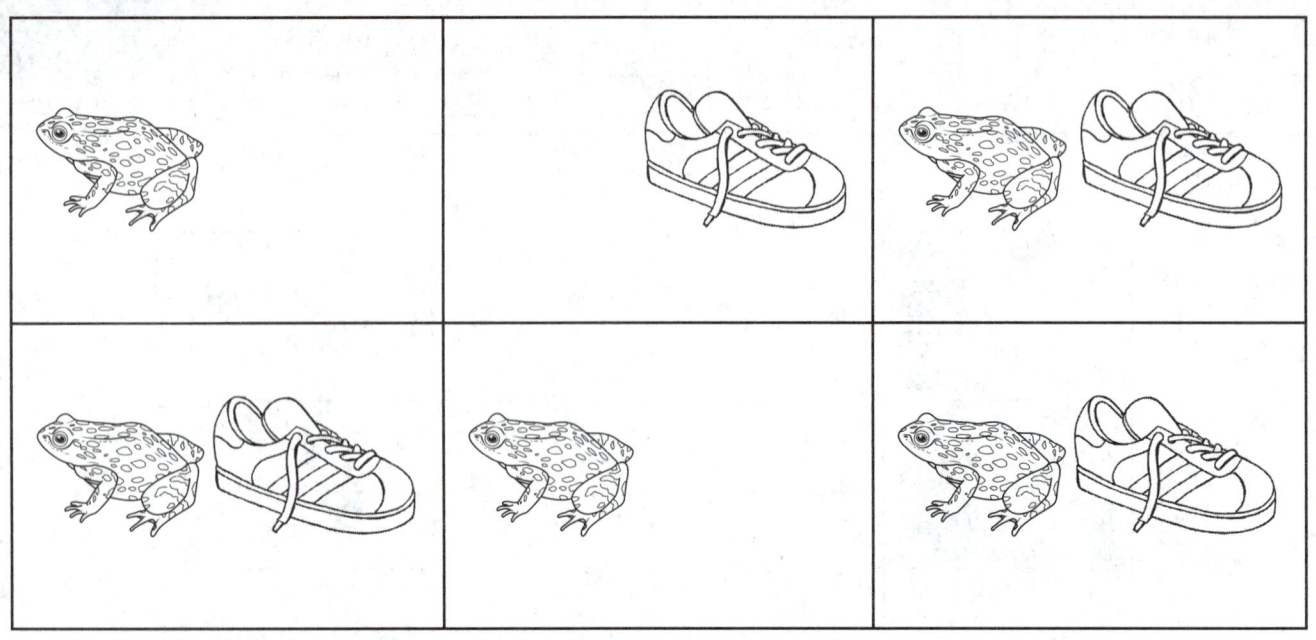

Side 2

50

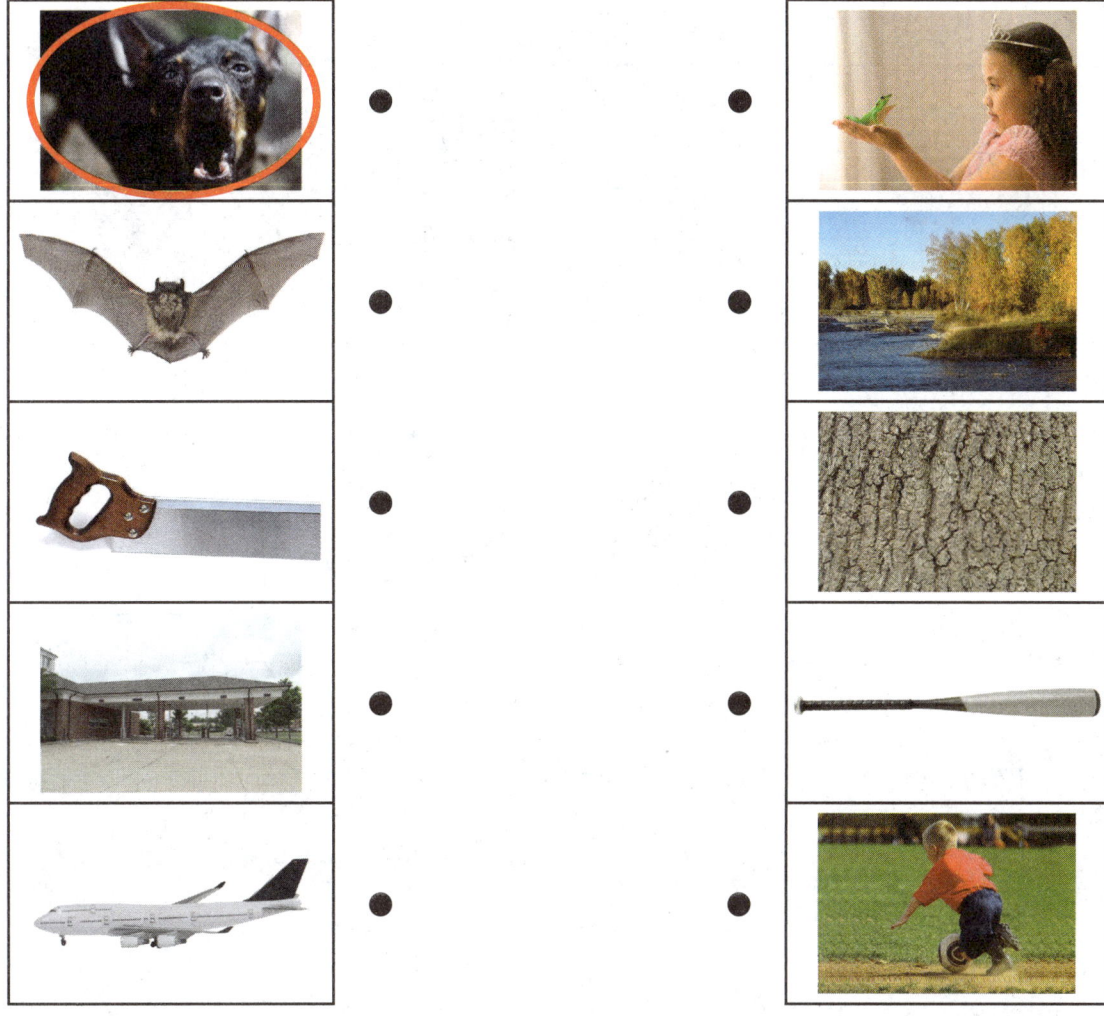

Side 1

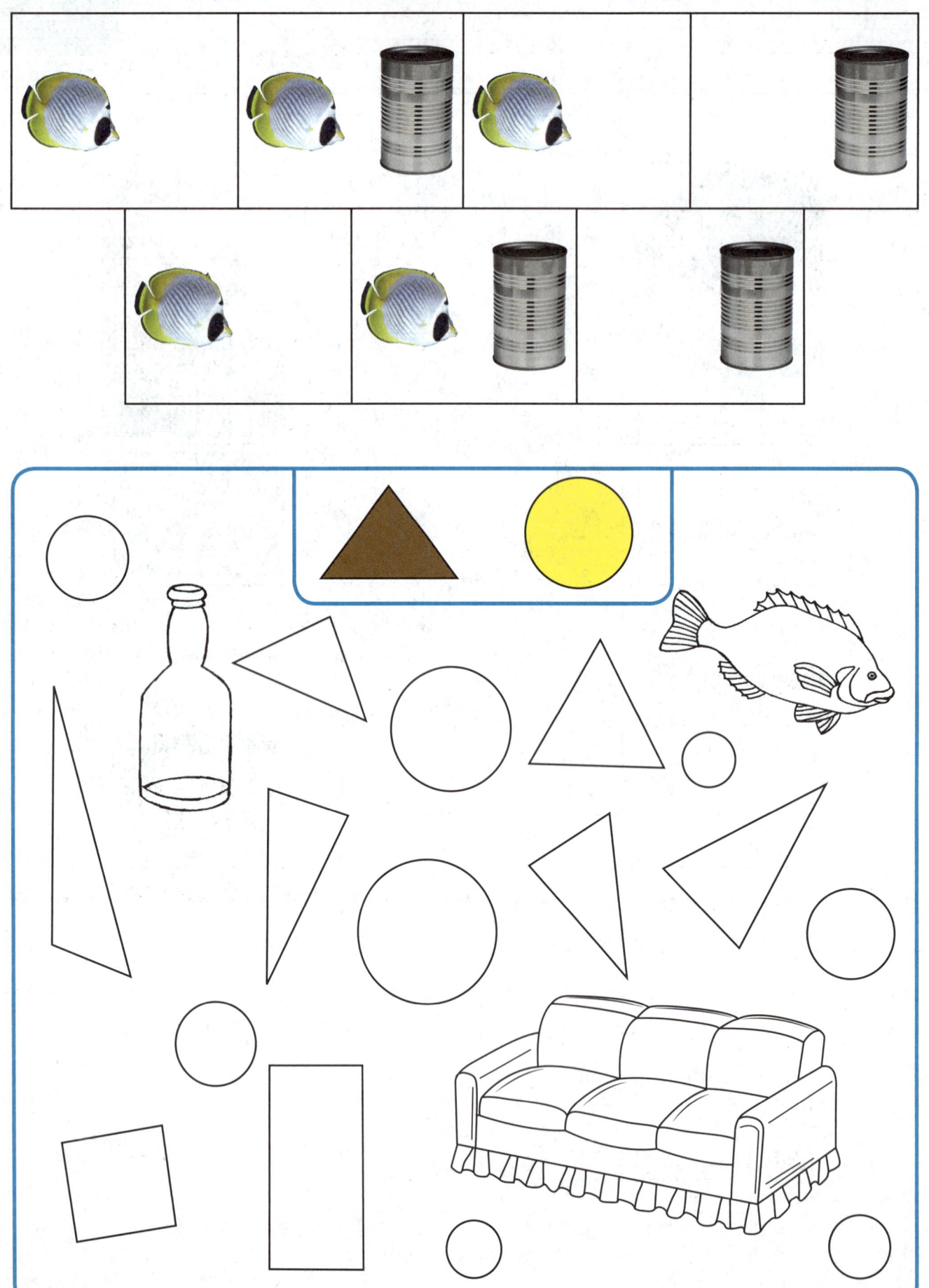

Side 2

51

Side 1

Side 2

52

Side 1

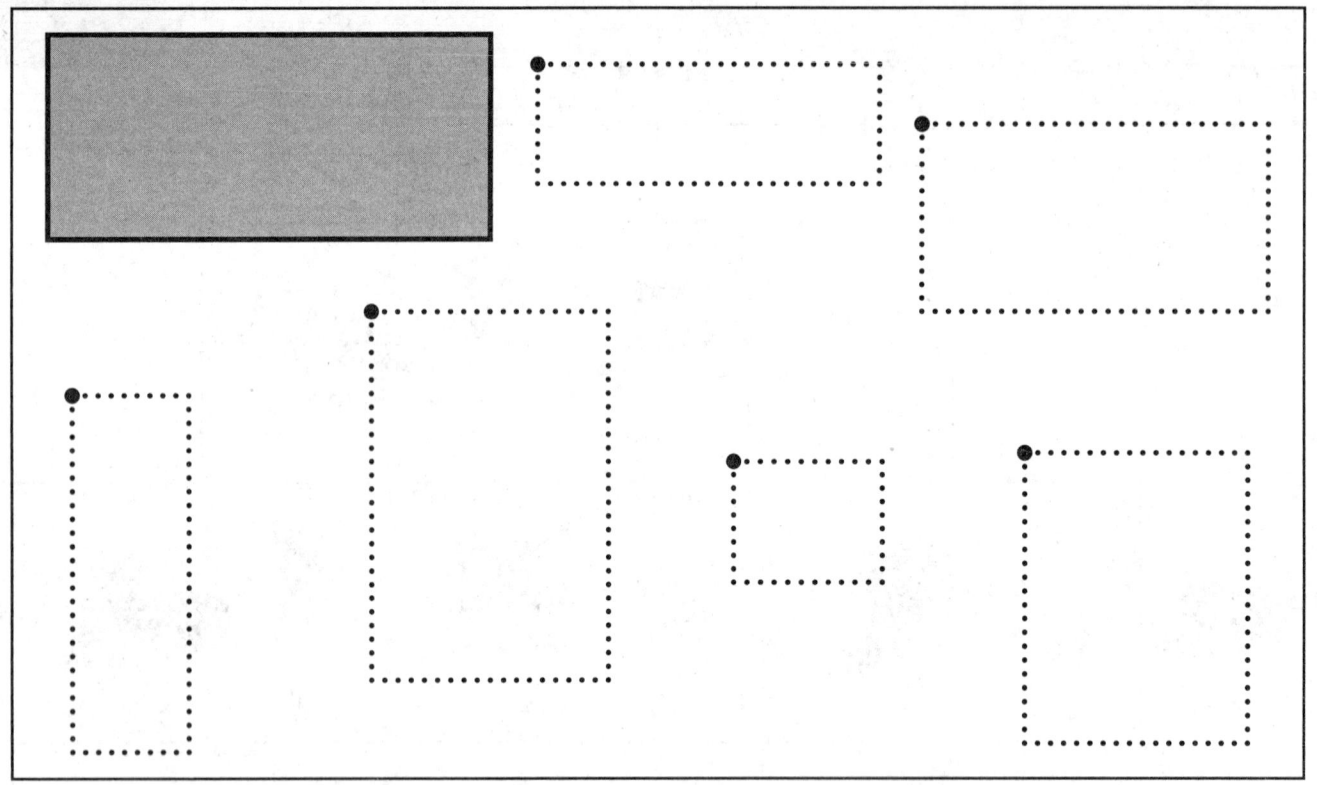

Side 2

53

Side 1

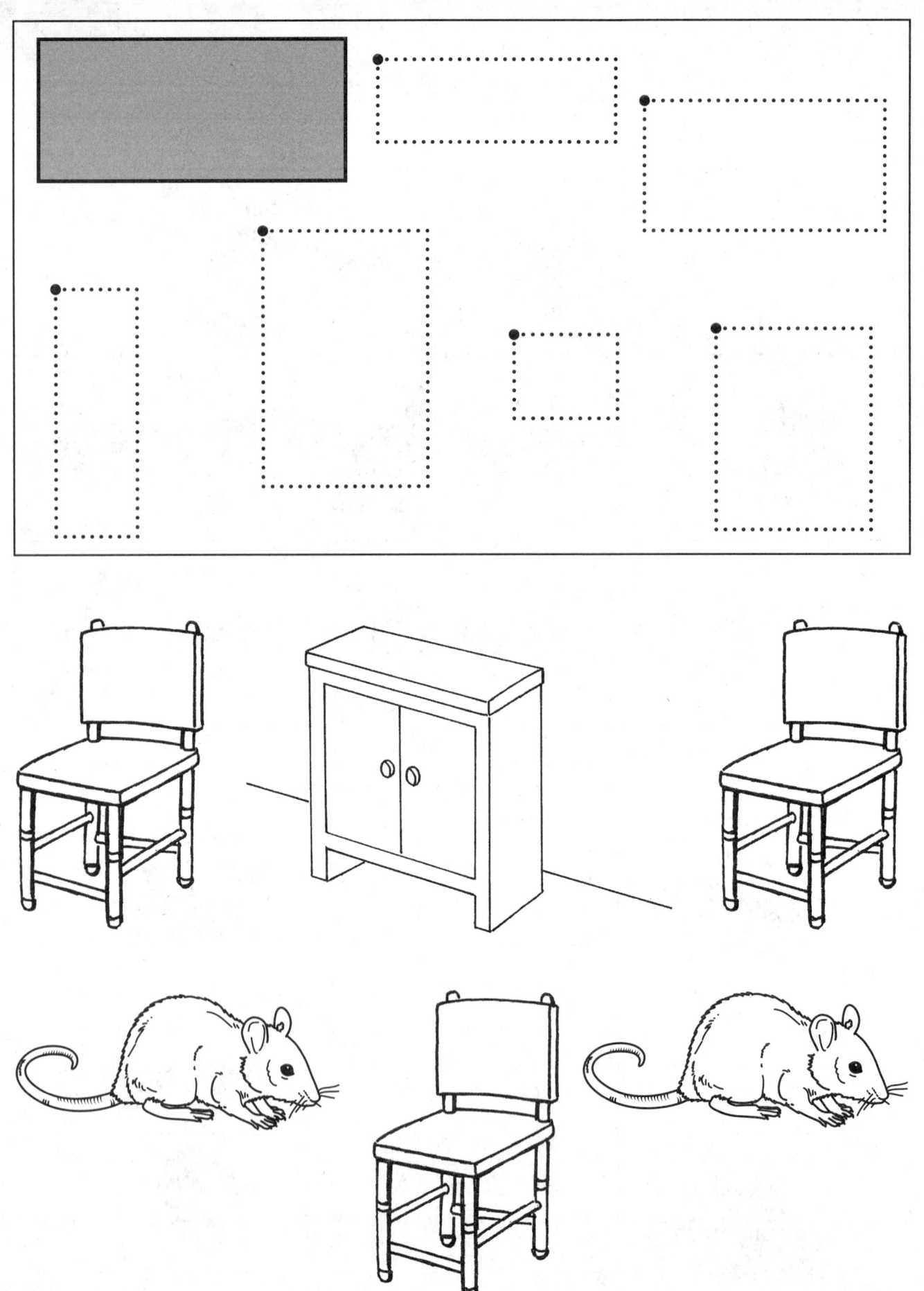

Side 2

54

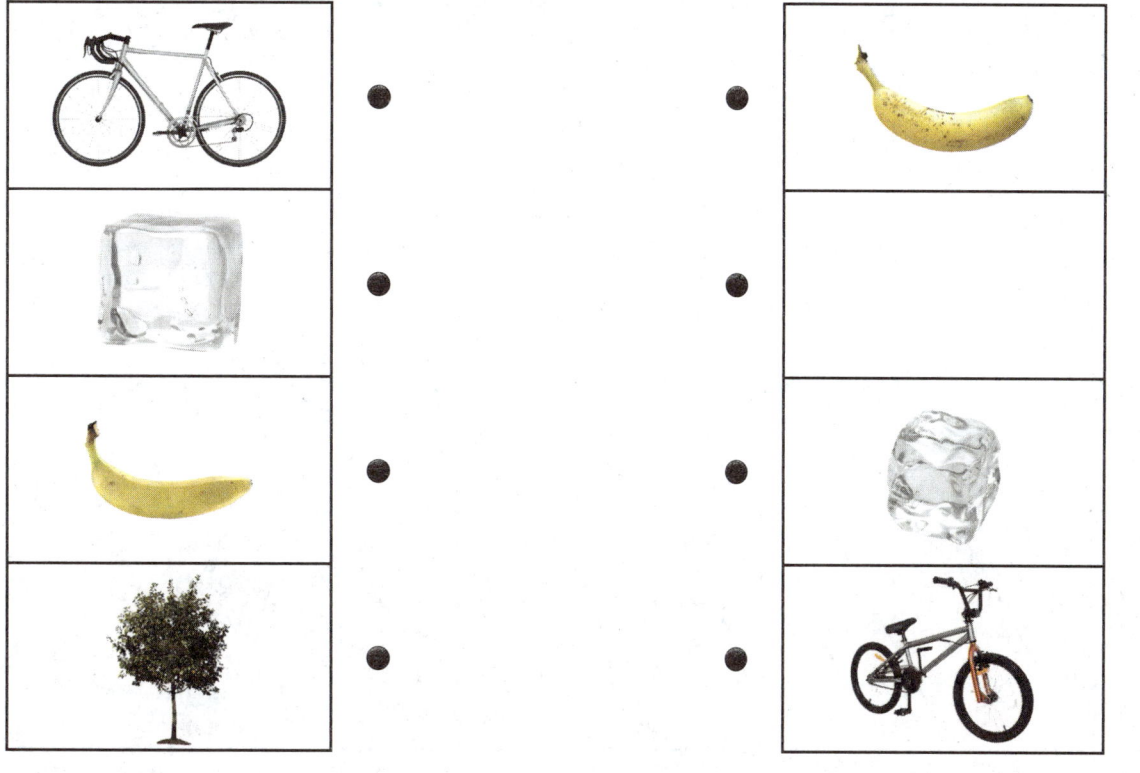

Side 1

Side 2

55

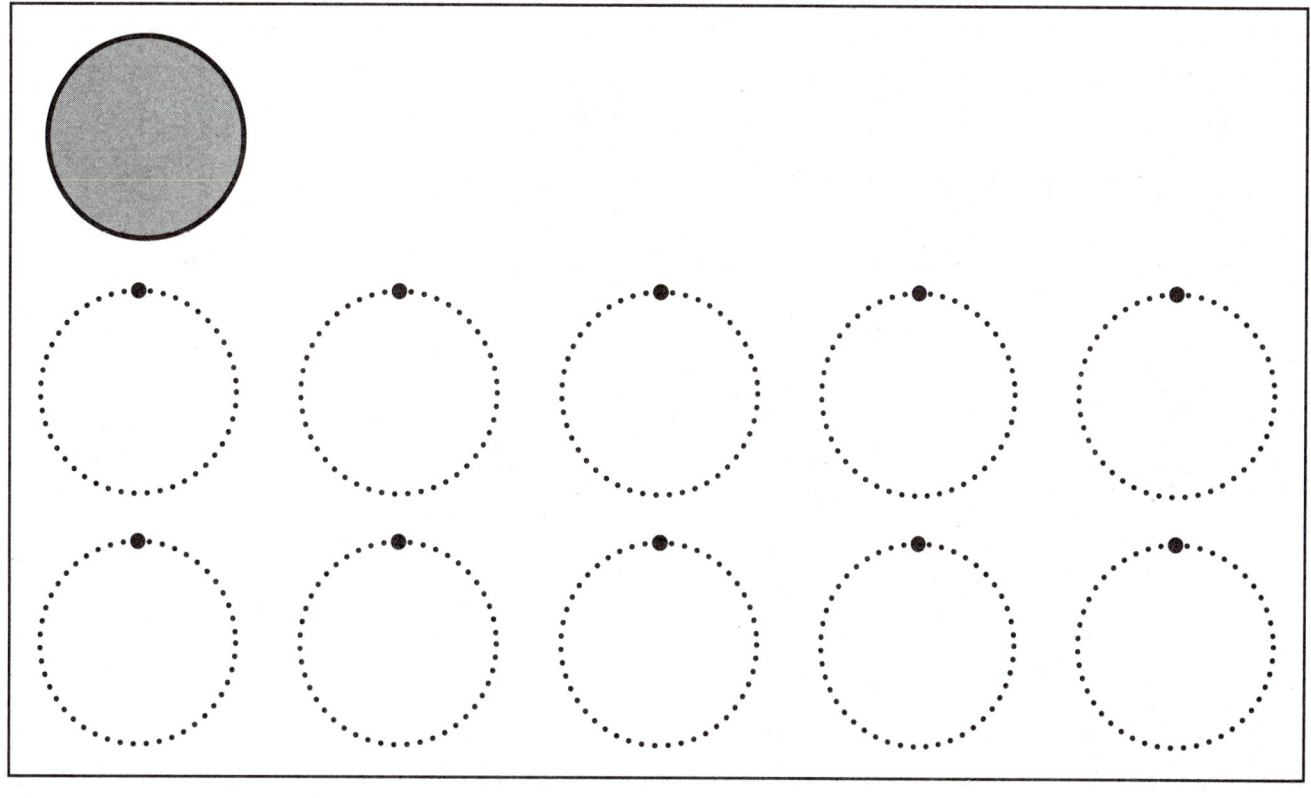

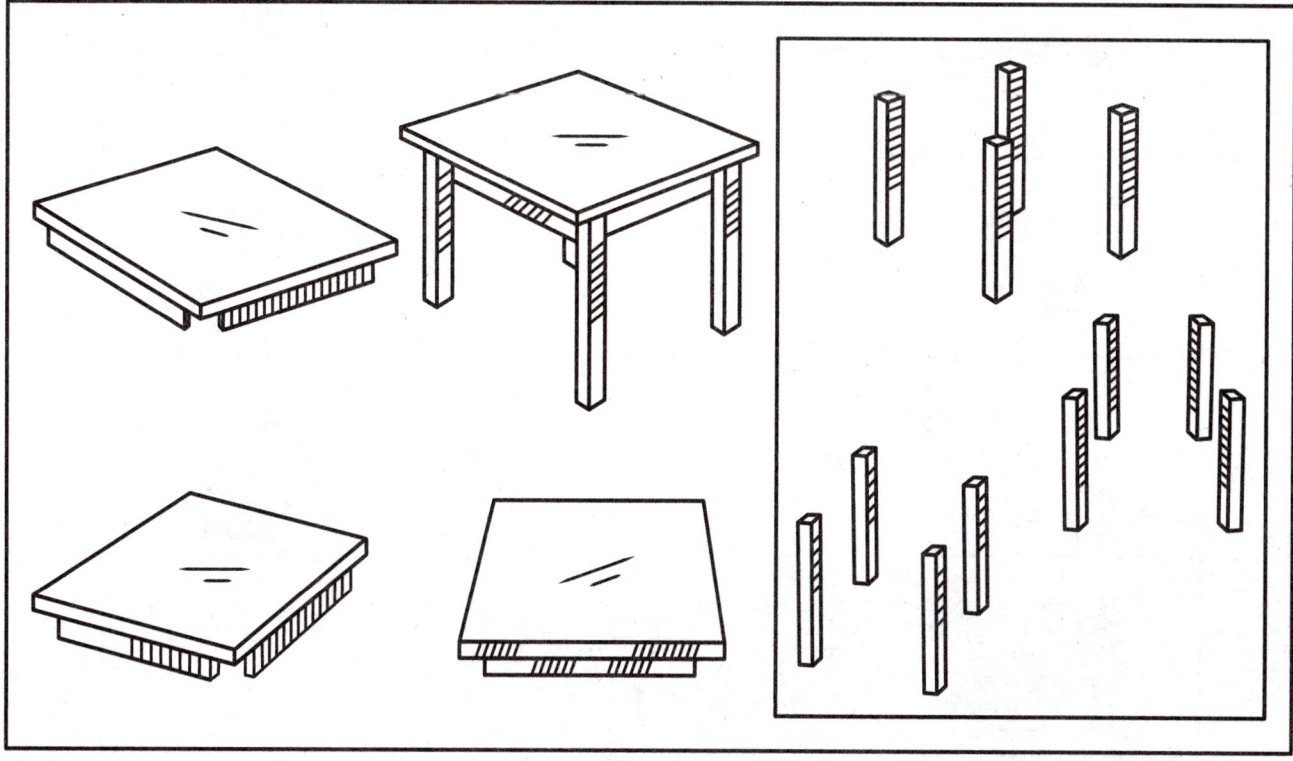

Side 1

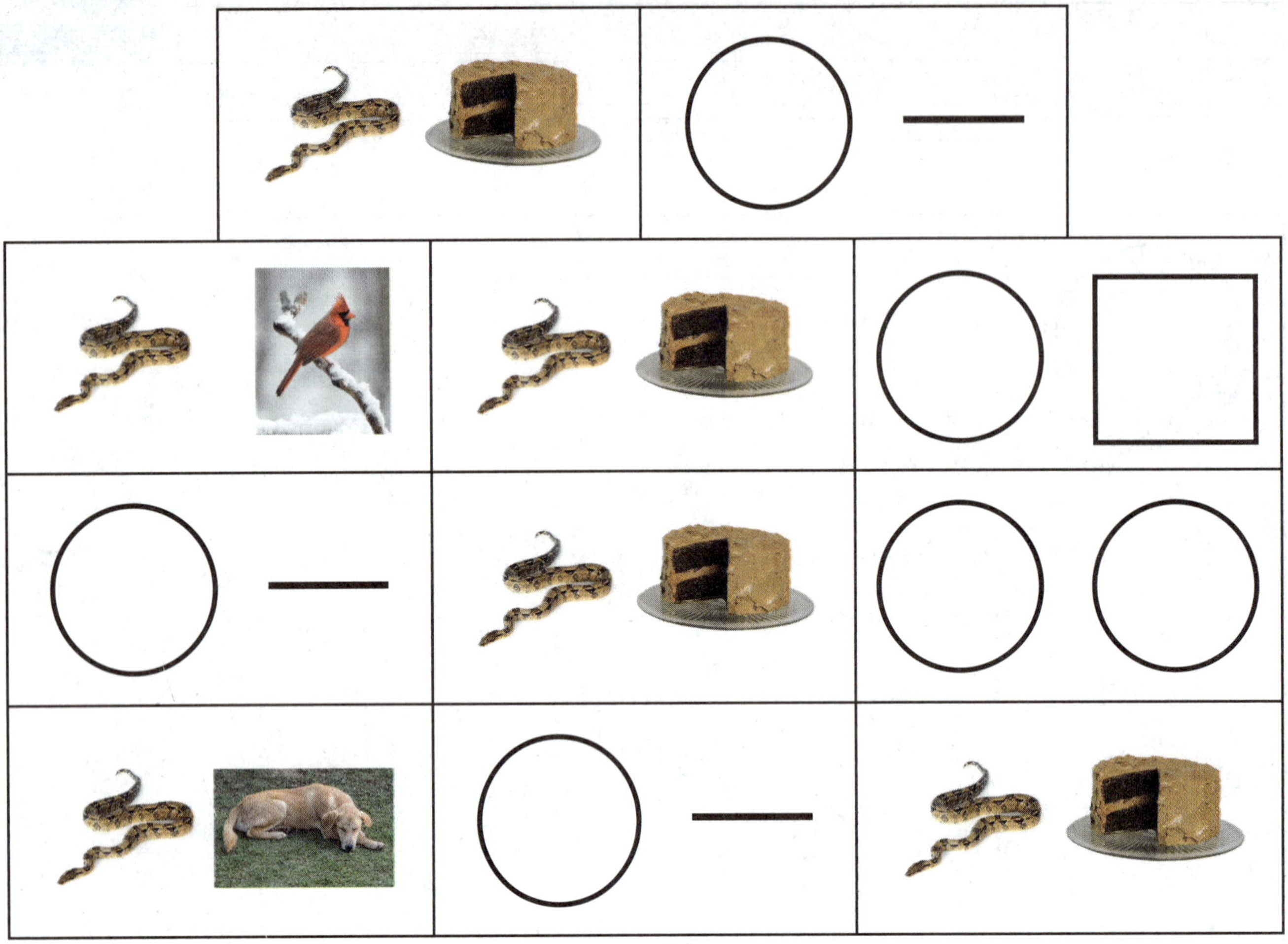

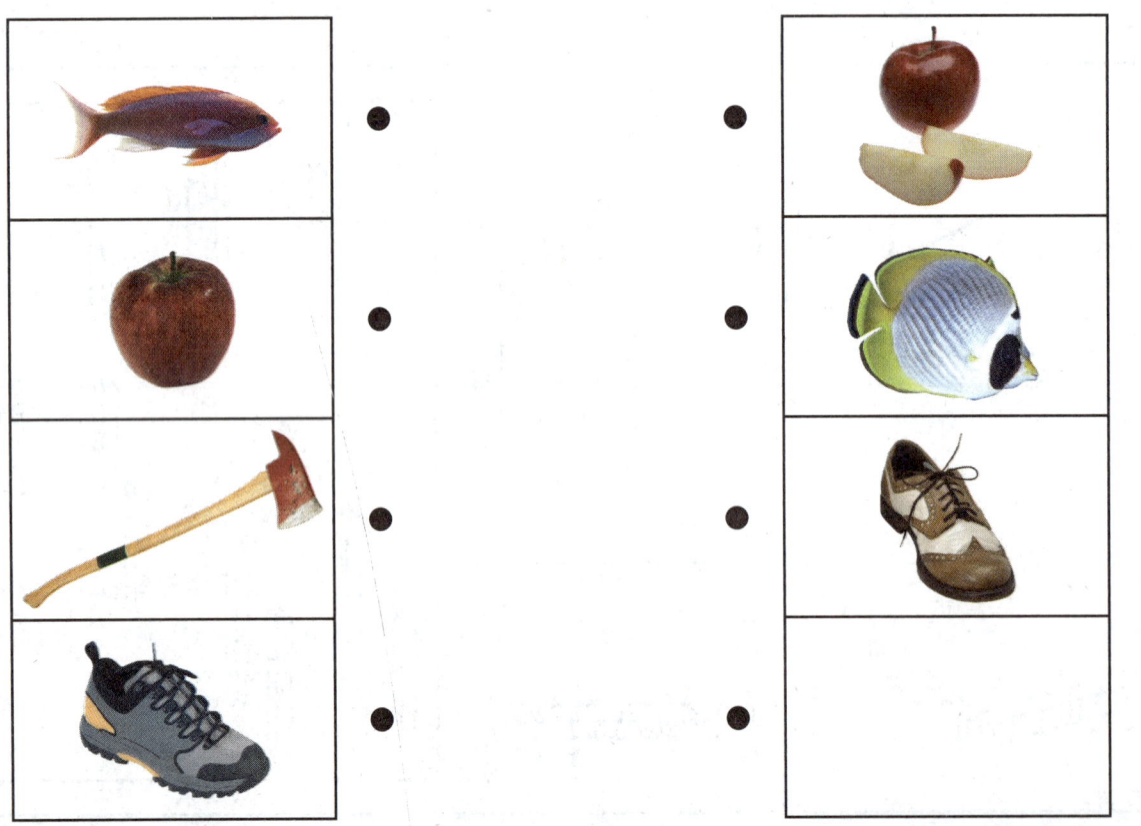

Side 2

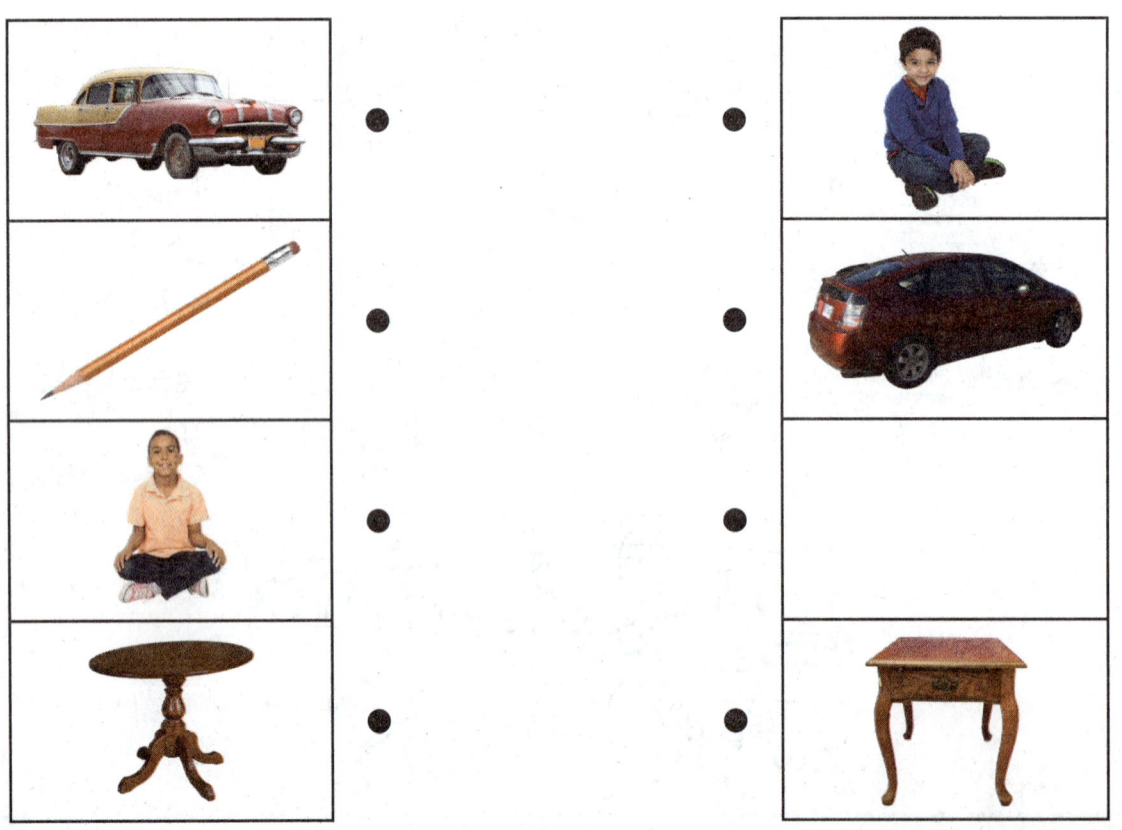

Side 2

57

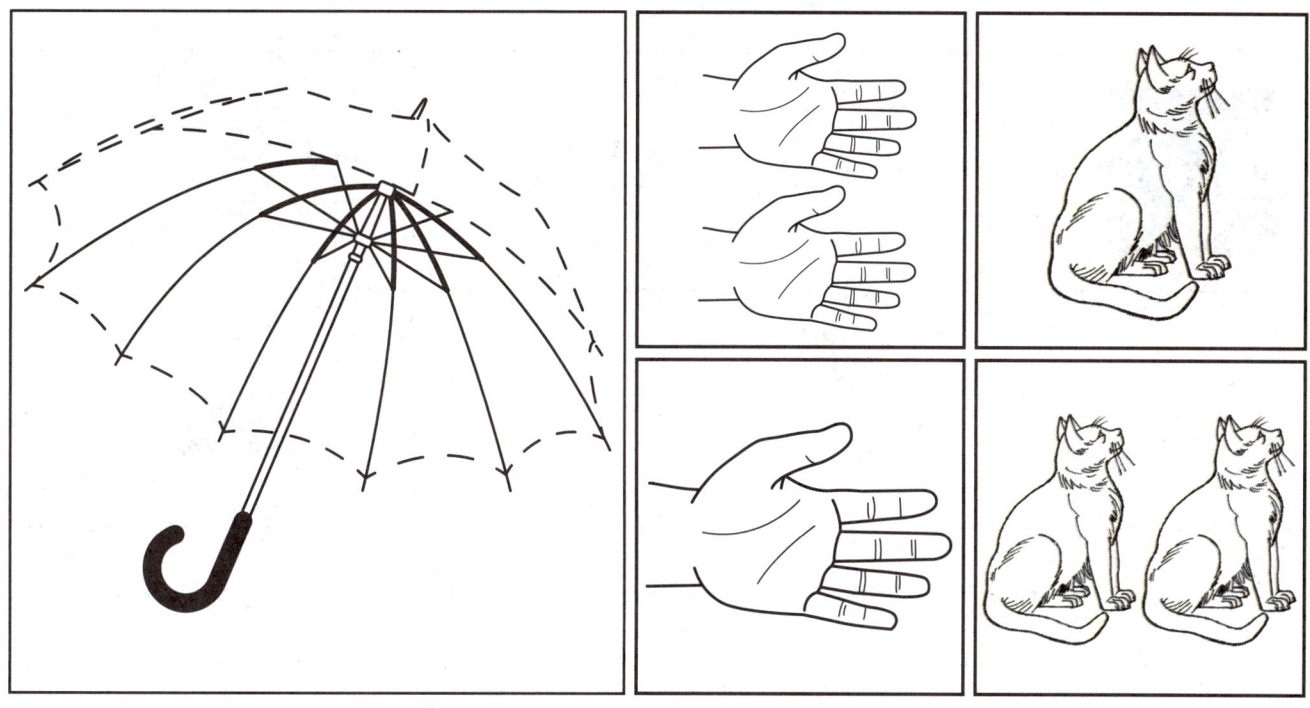

Side 1

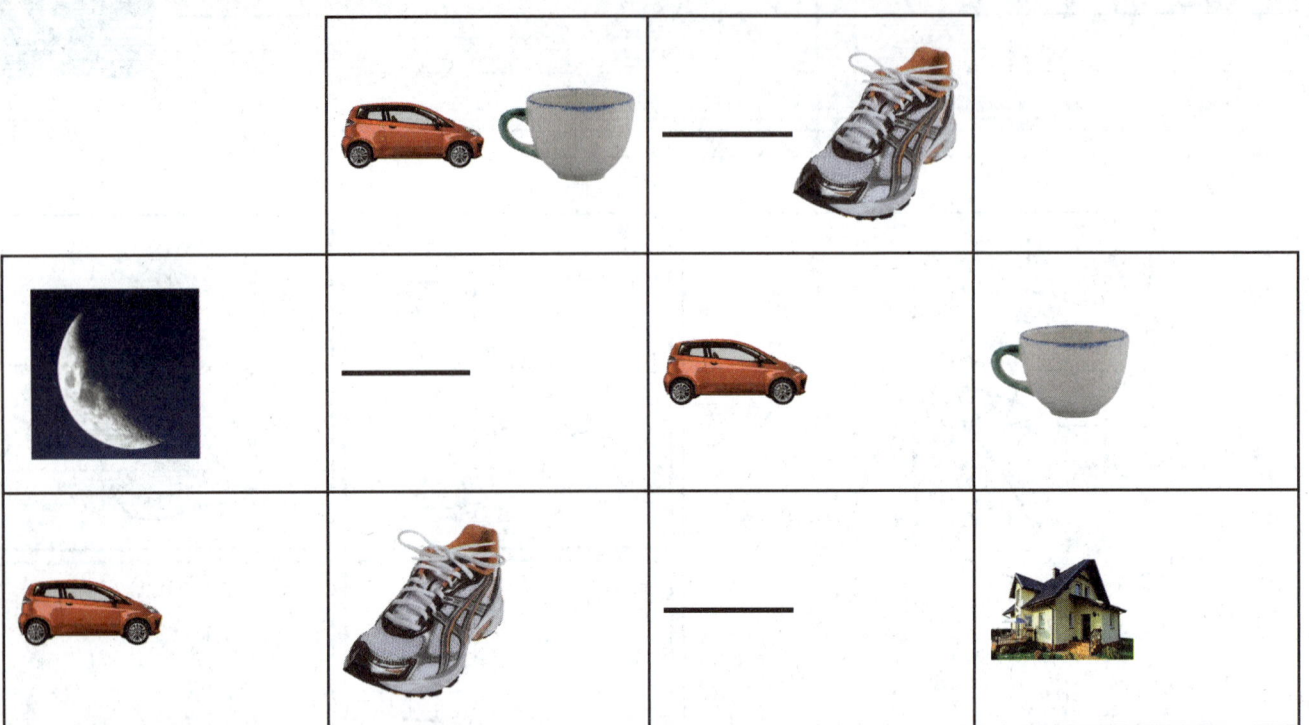

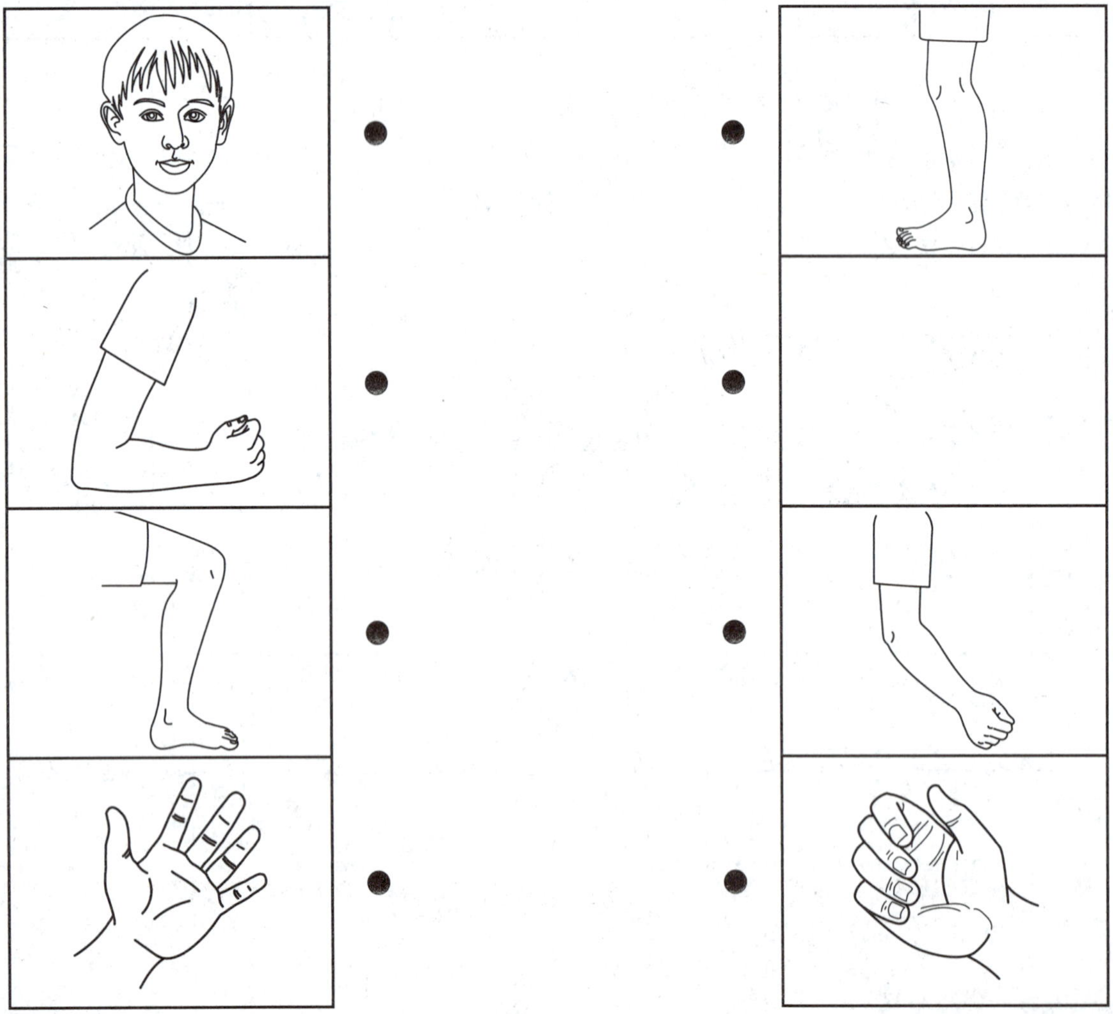

Side 2

58

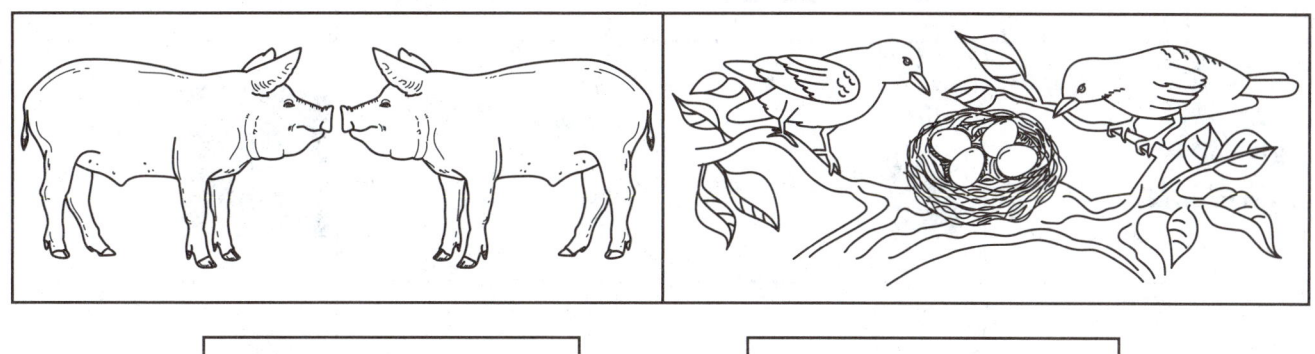

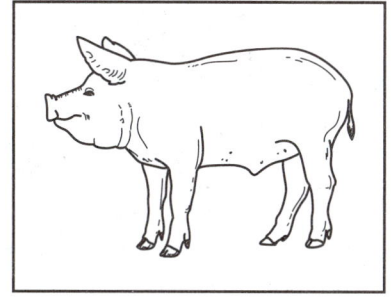

Side 1

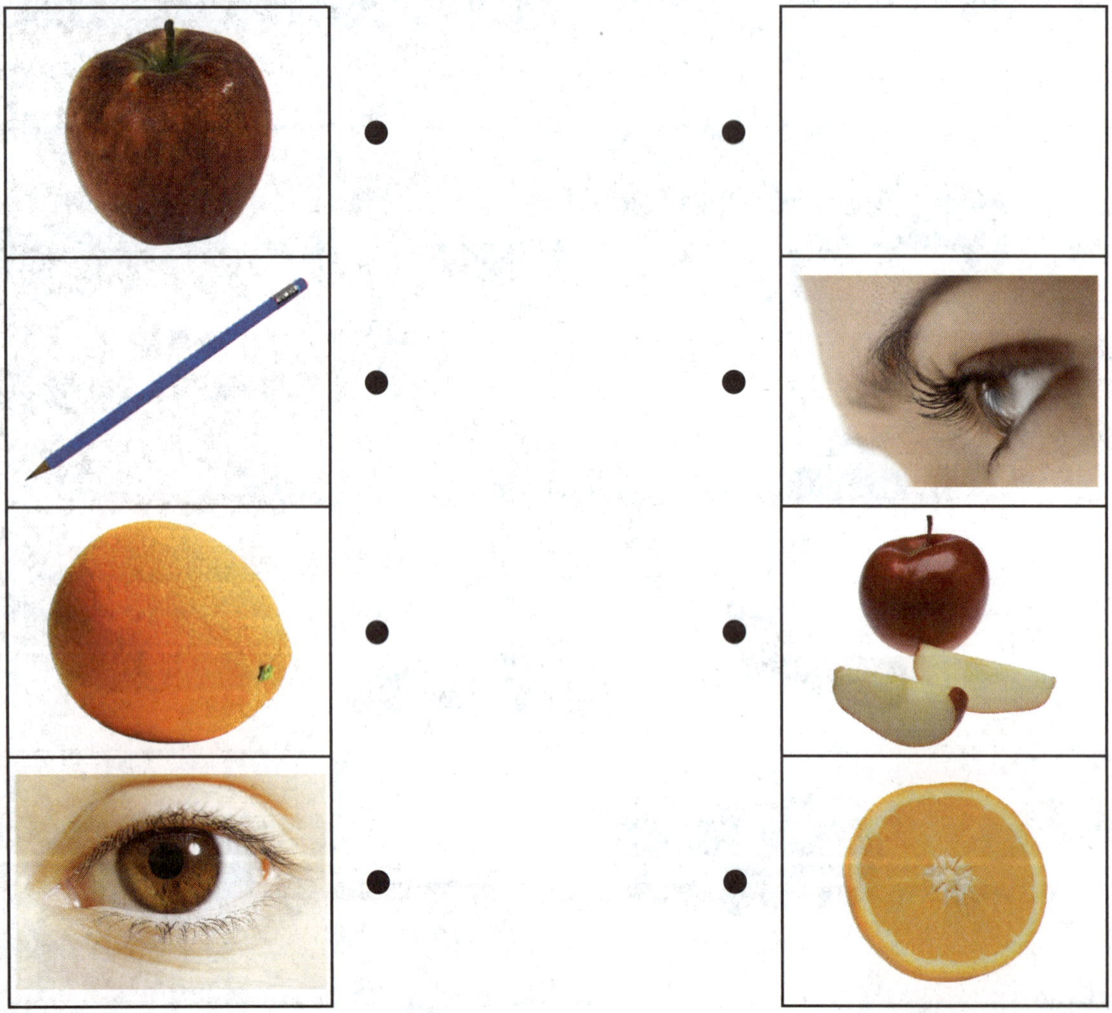

Side 2

59

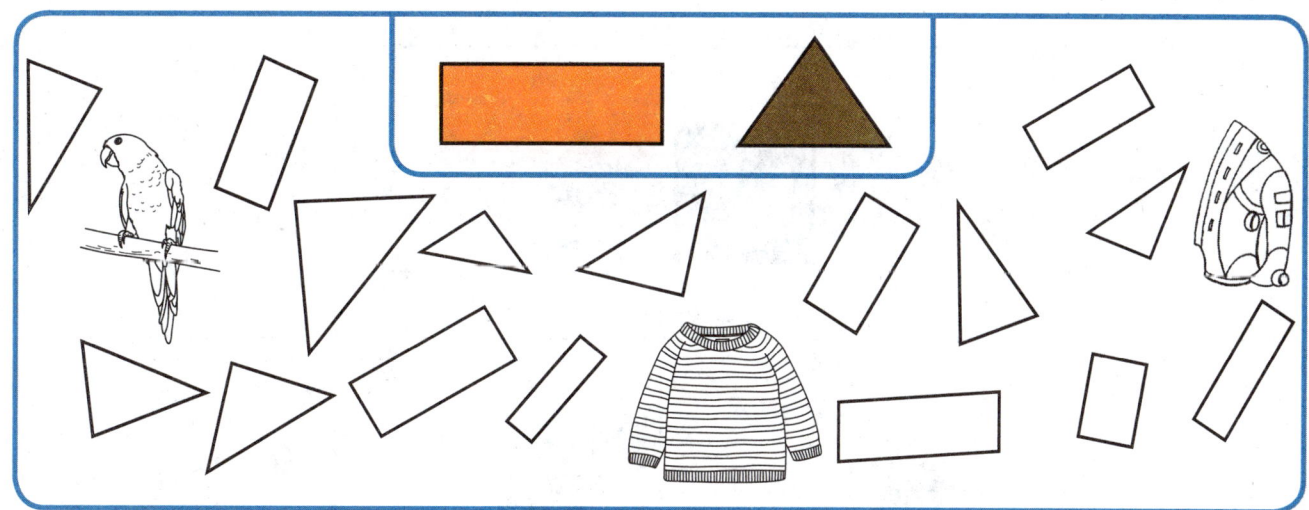

Side 1

Side 2

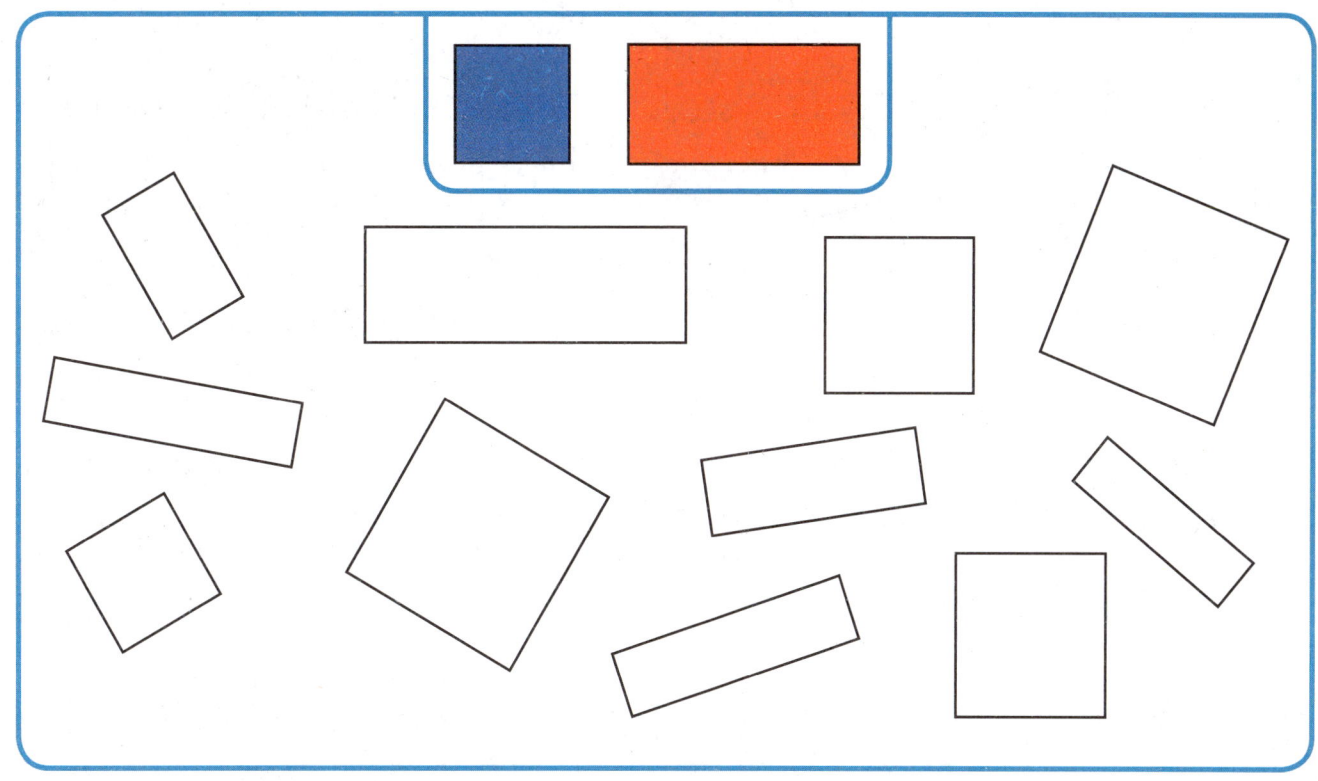

Side 1

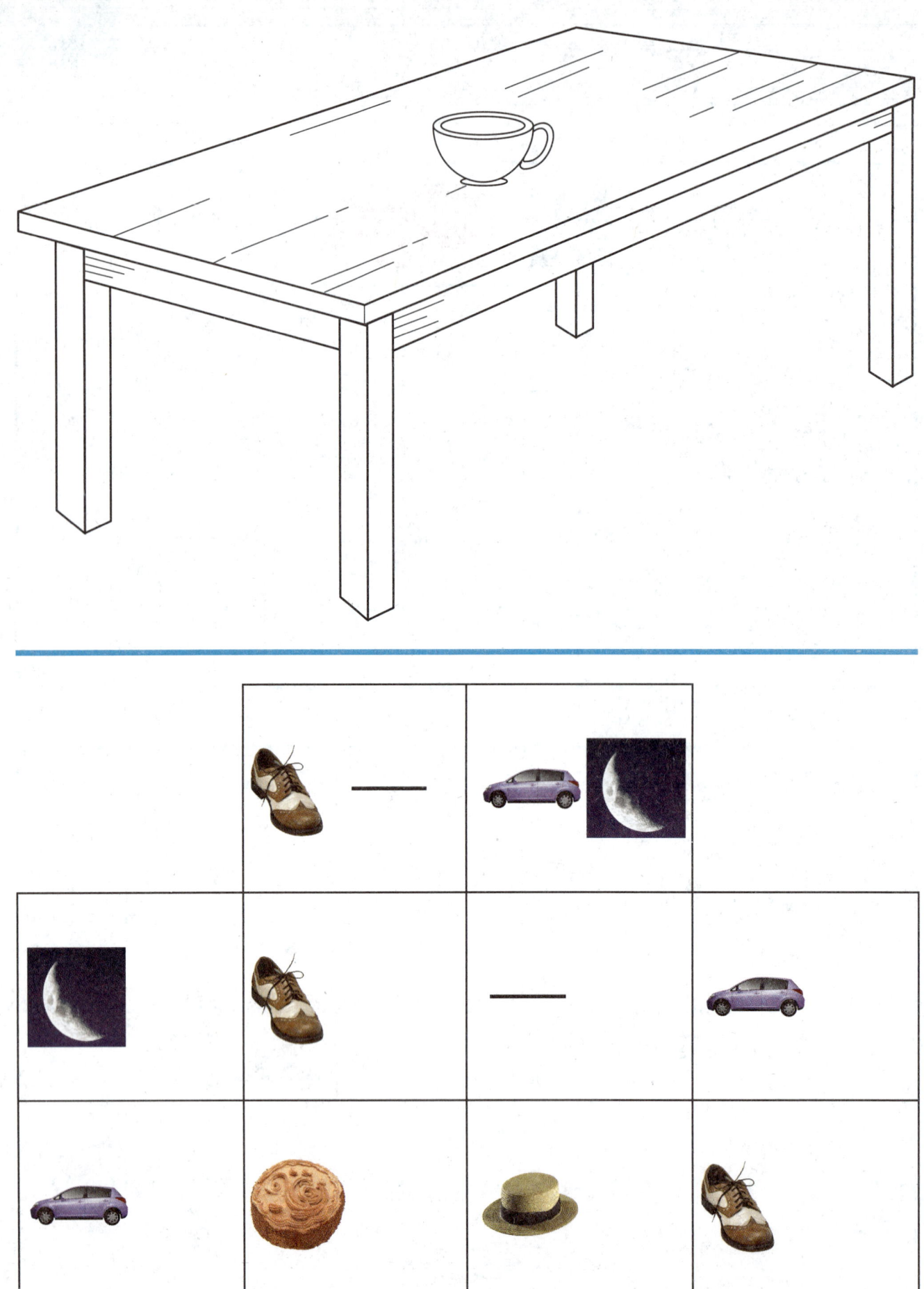

Side 2

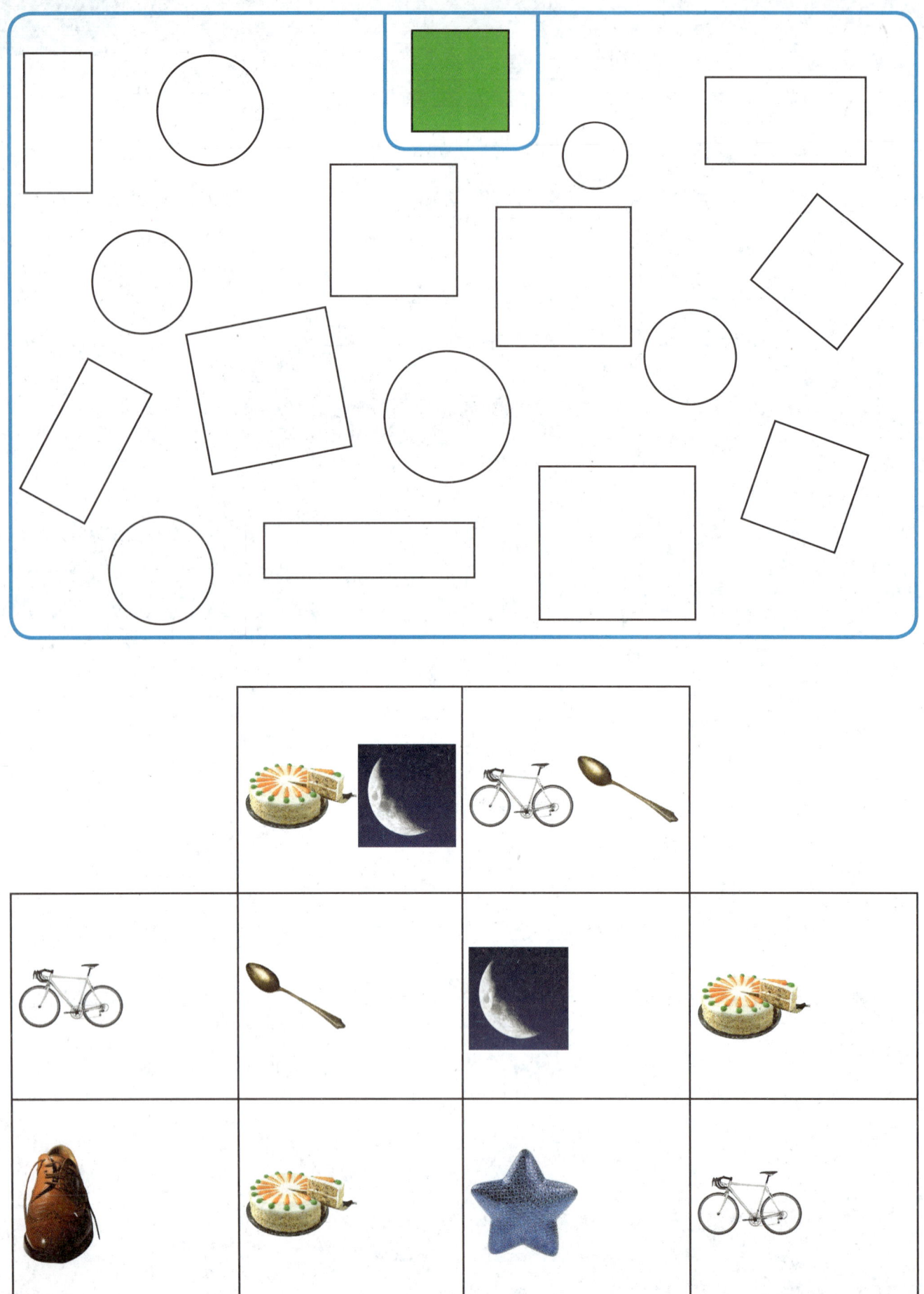

Side 2

62

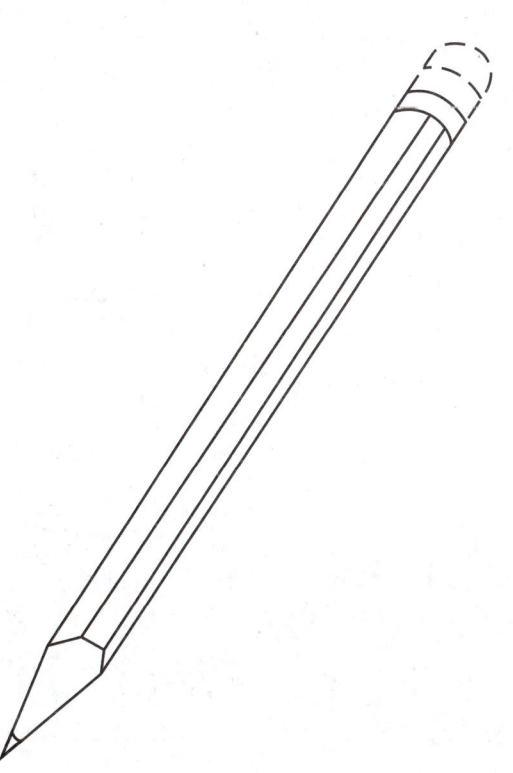
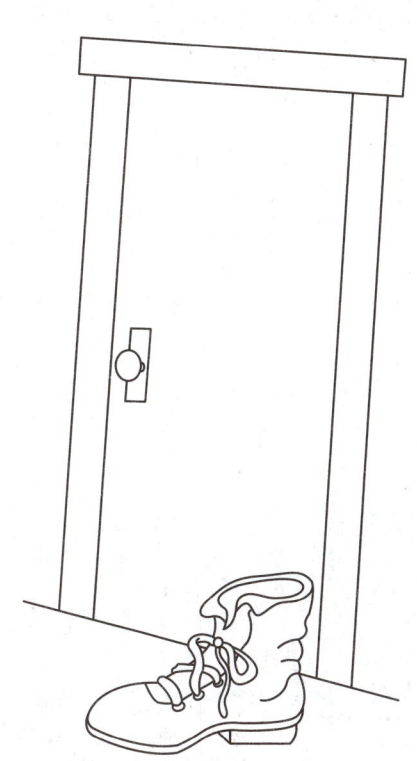

Side 1

Side 2

63

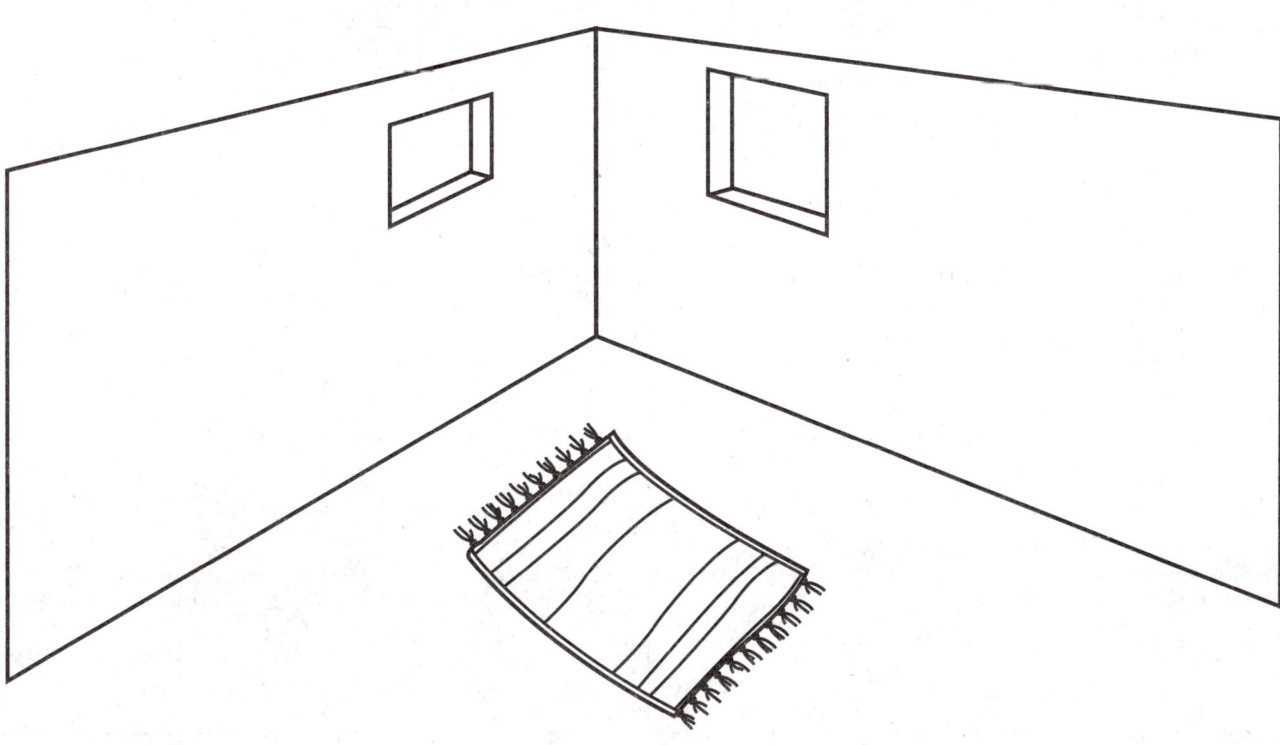

Side 1

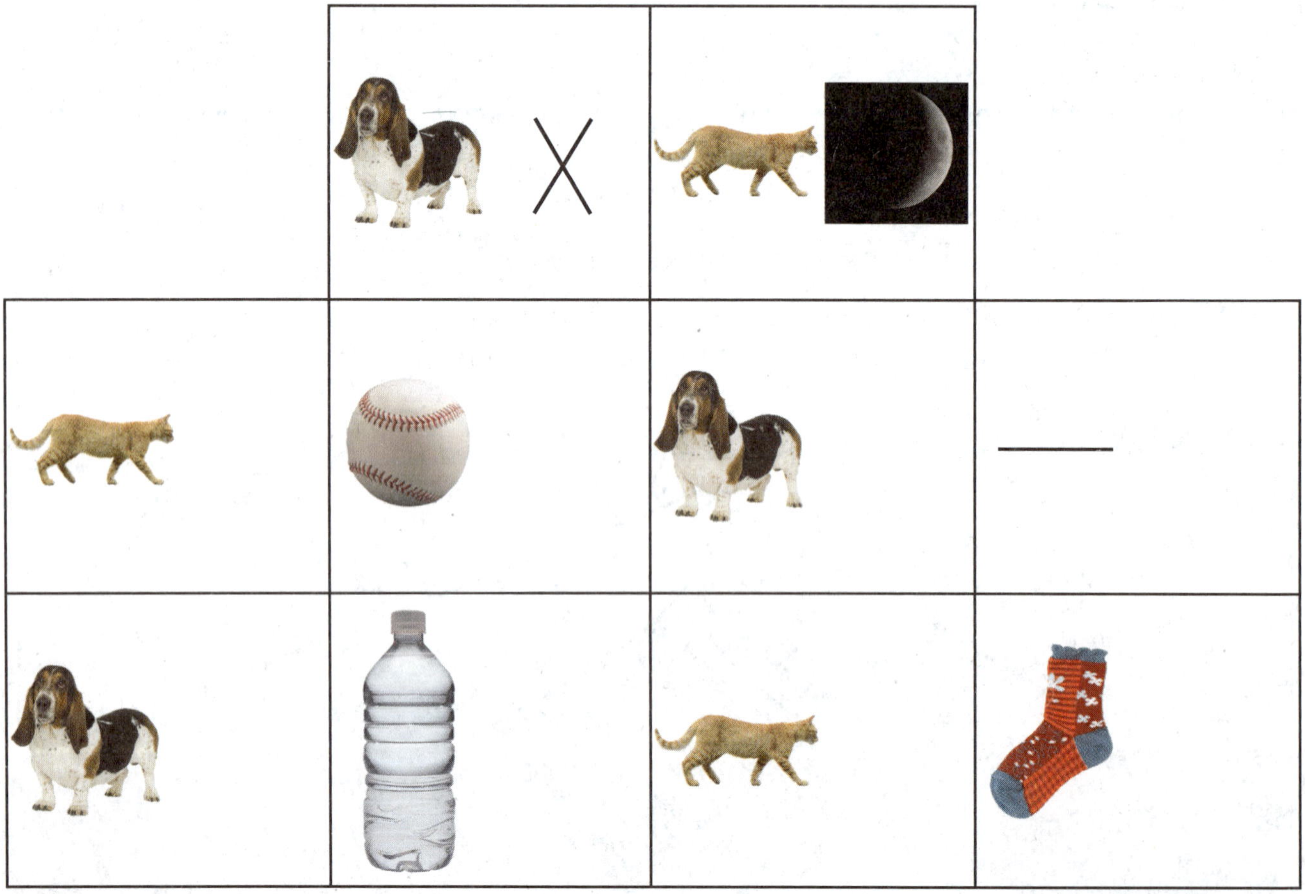

Side 2

64

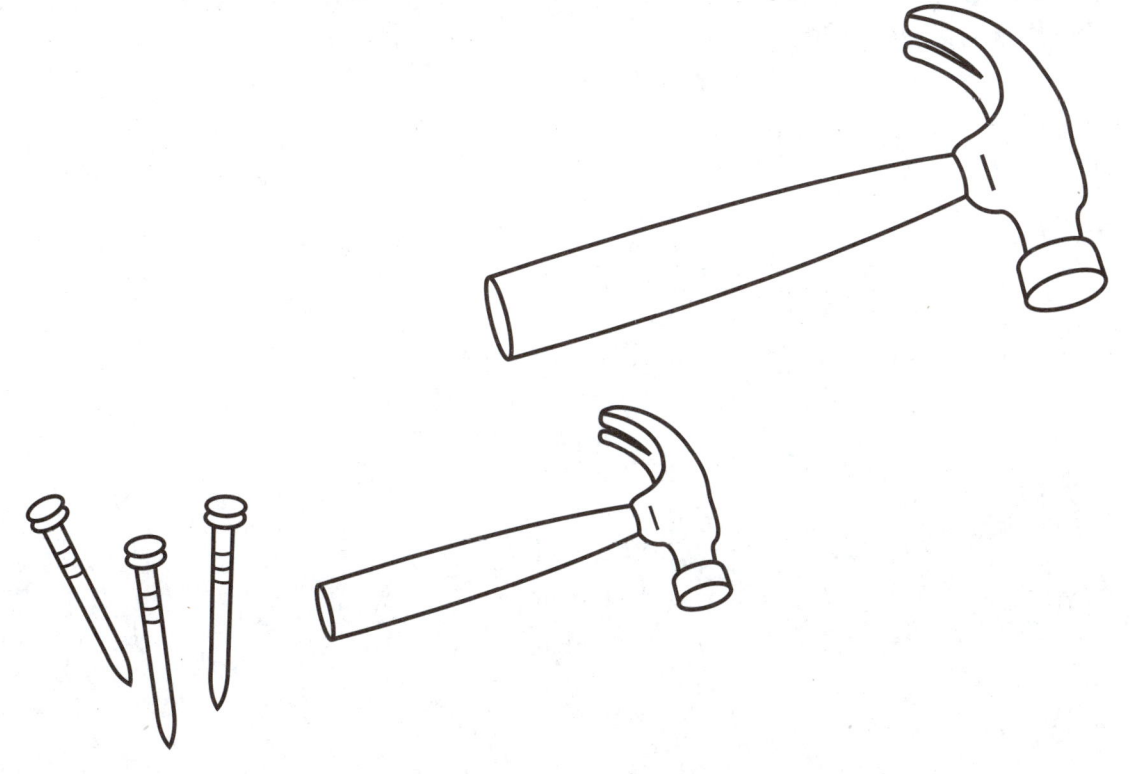

Side 1

Side 2

65

Side 1

Side 2

66

Side 1

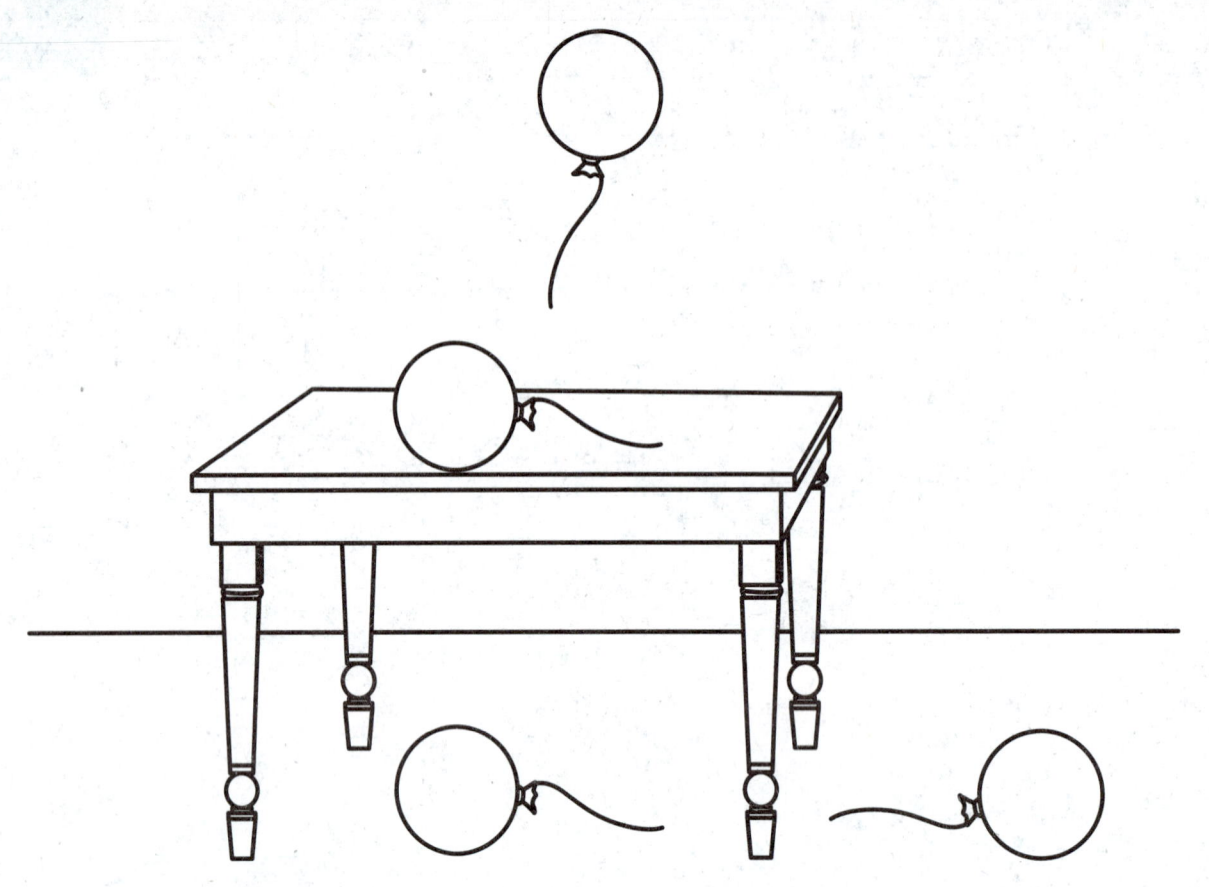

Side 2

67

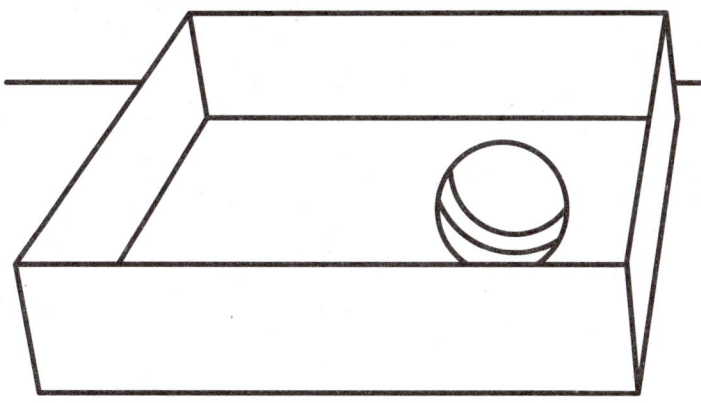

Side 1

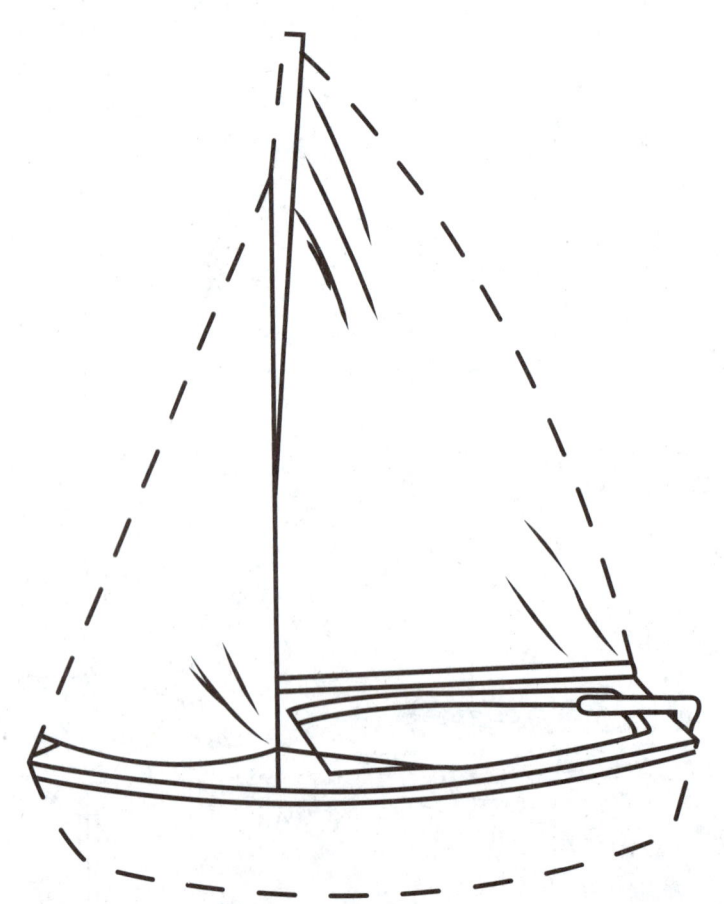

Side 2

68

Side 1

Side 2

69

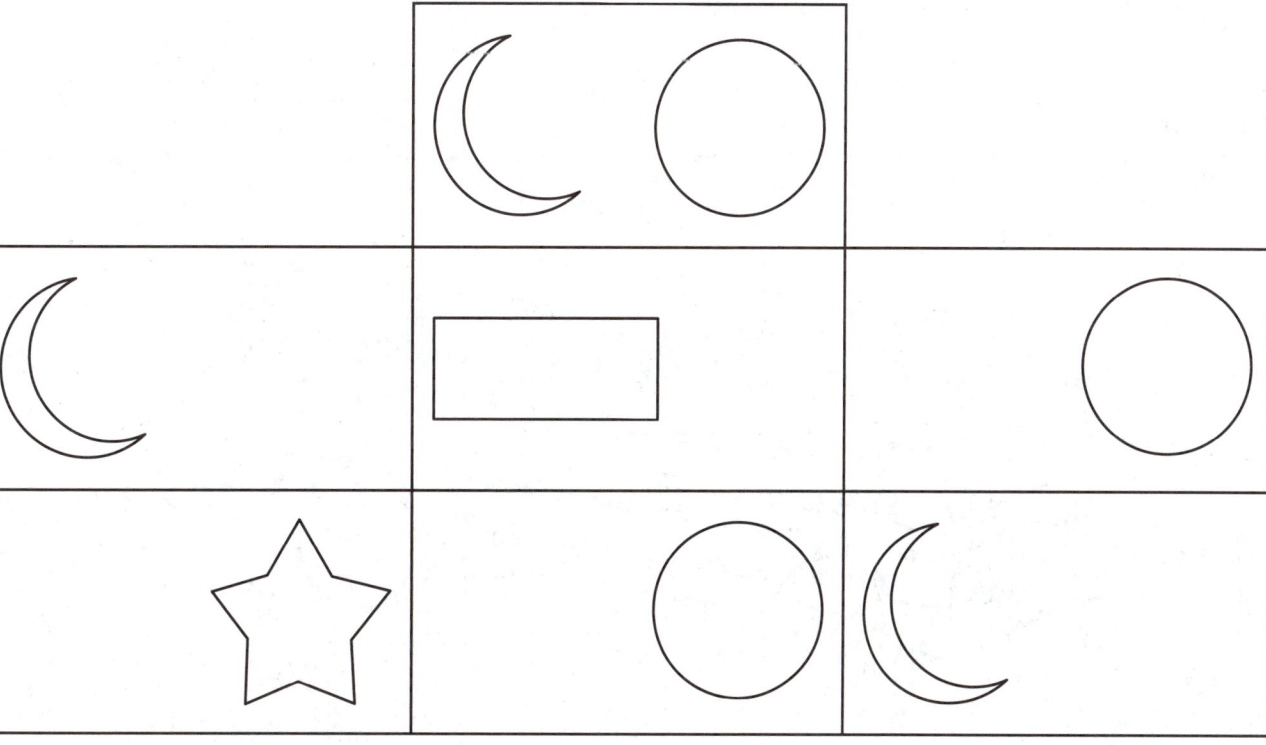

Side 1

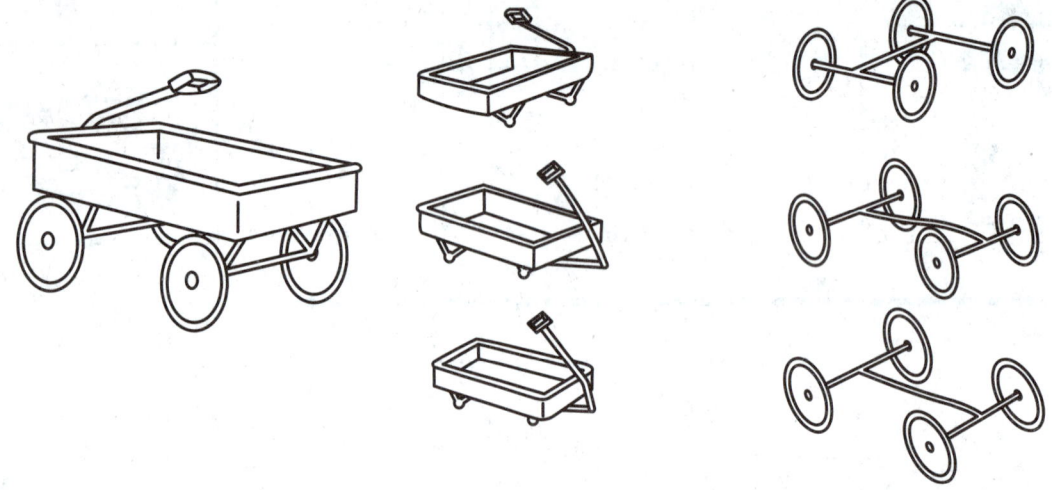

Side 2

70

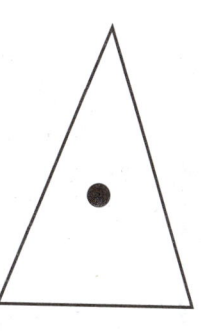

Side 1

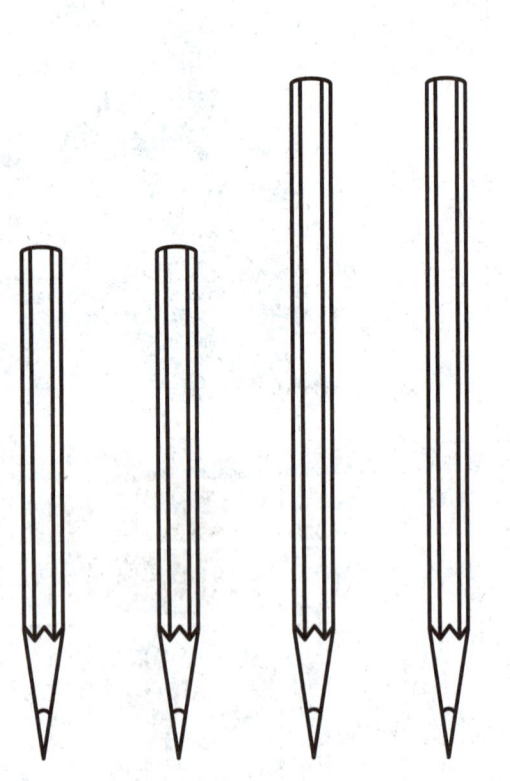

Side 2

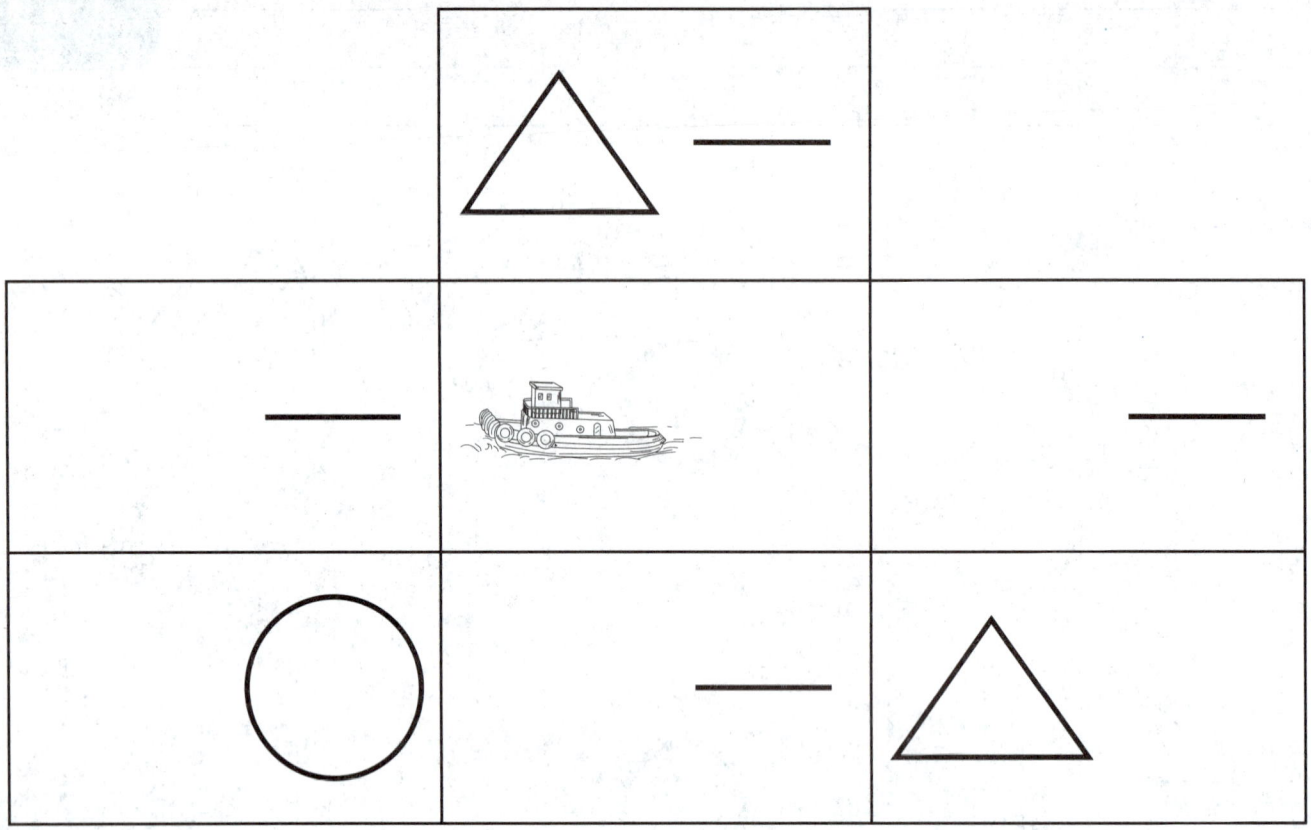

Side 2

72

Side 1

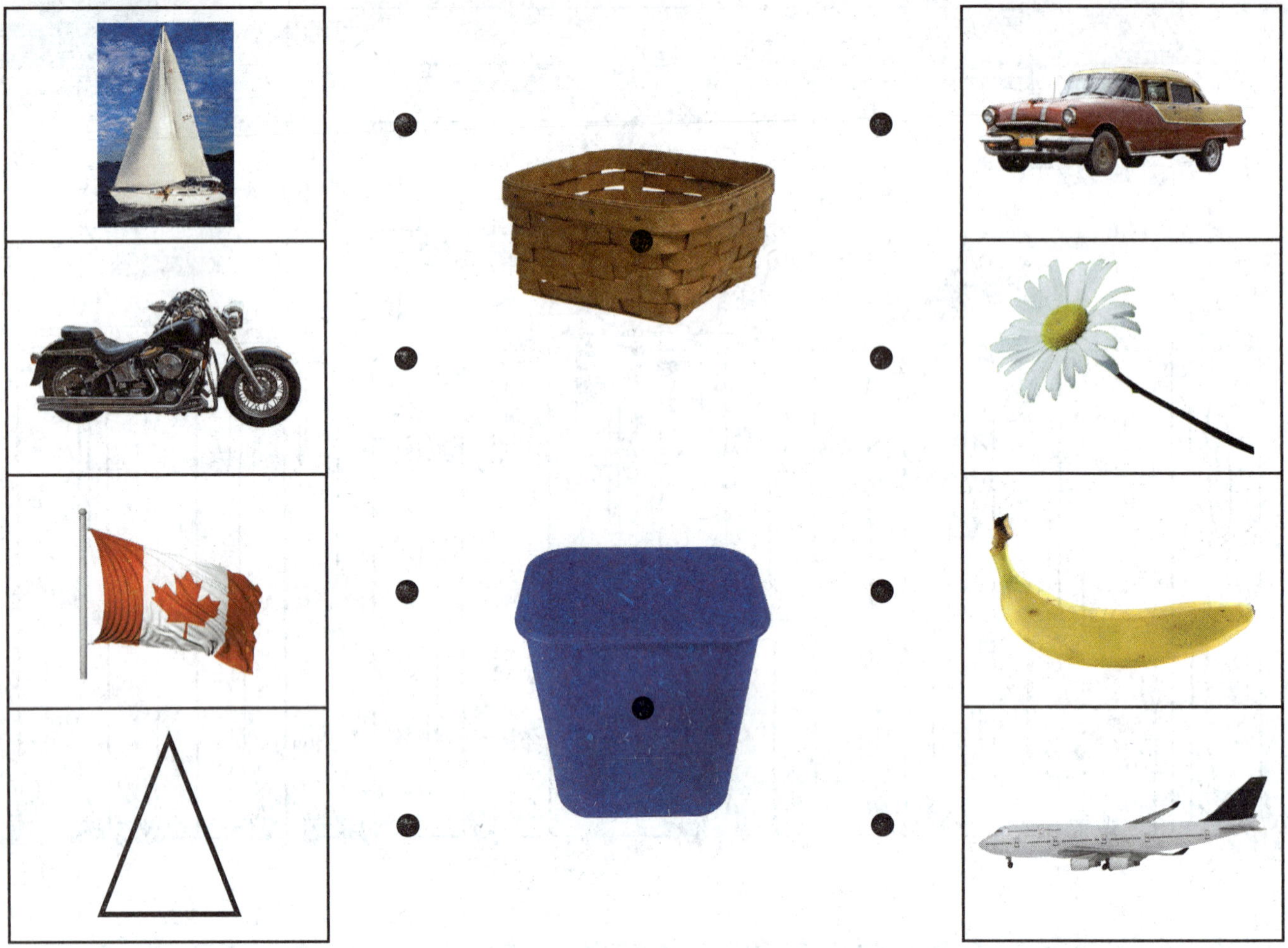

Side 2

73

Side 1

Side 2

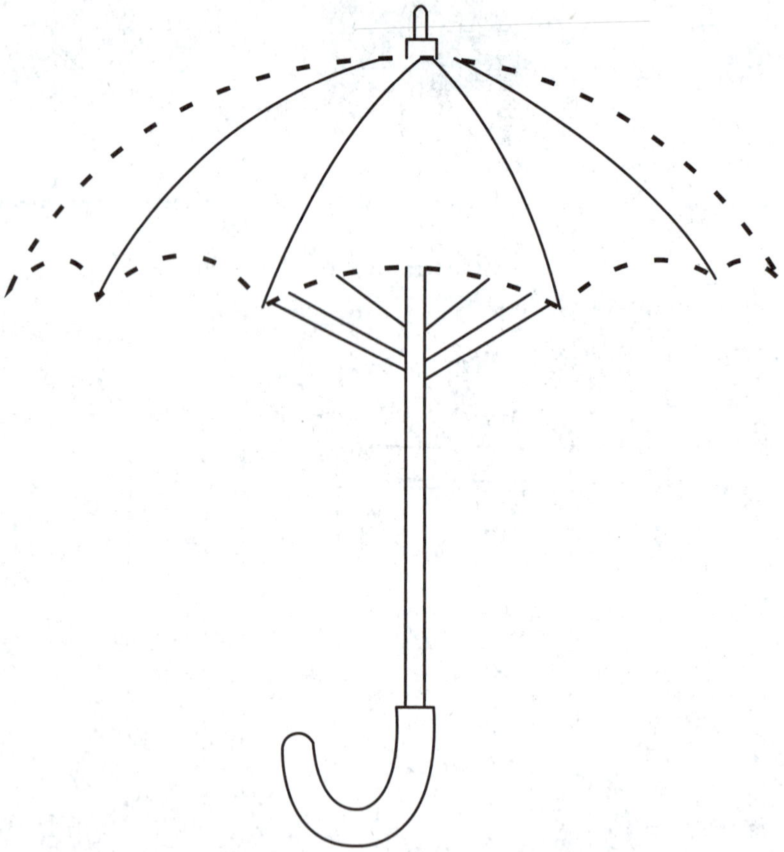

Side 2

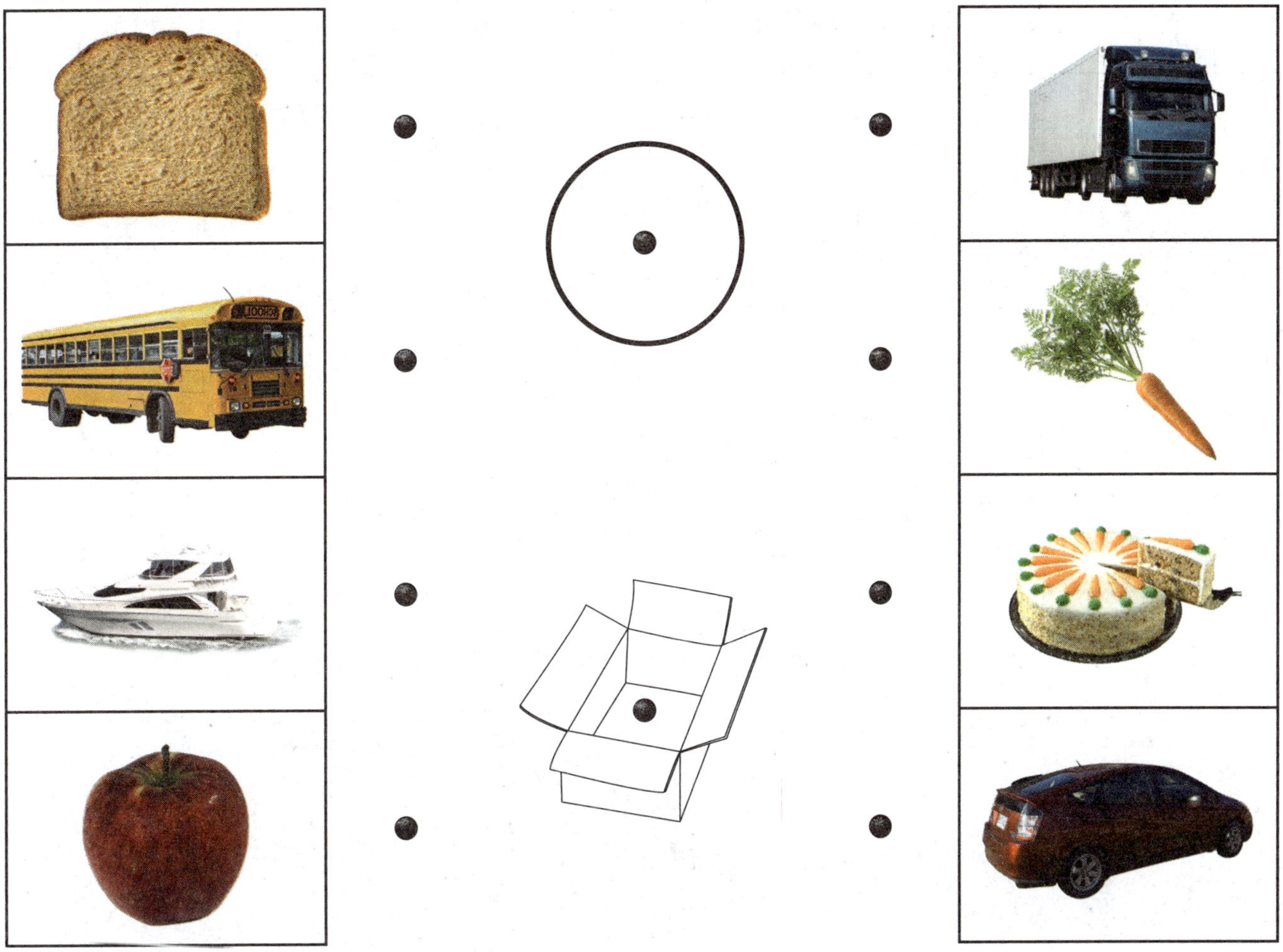

75

Side 1

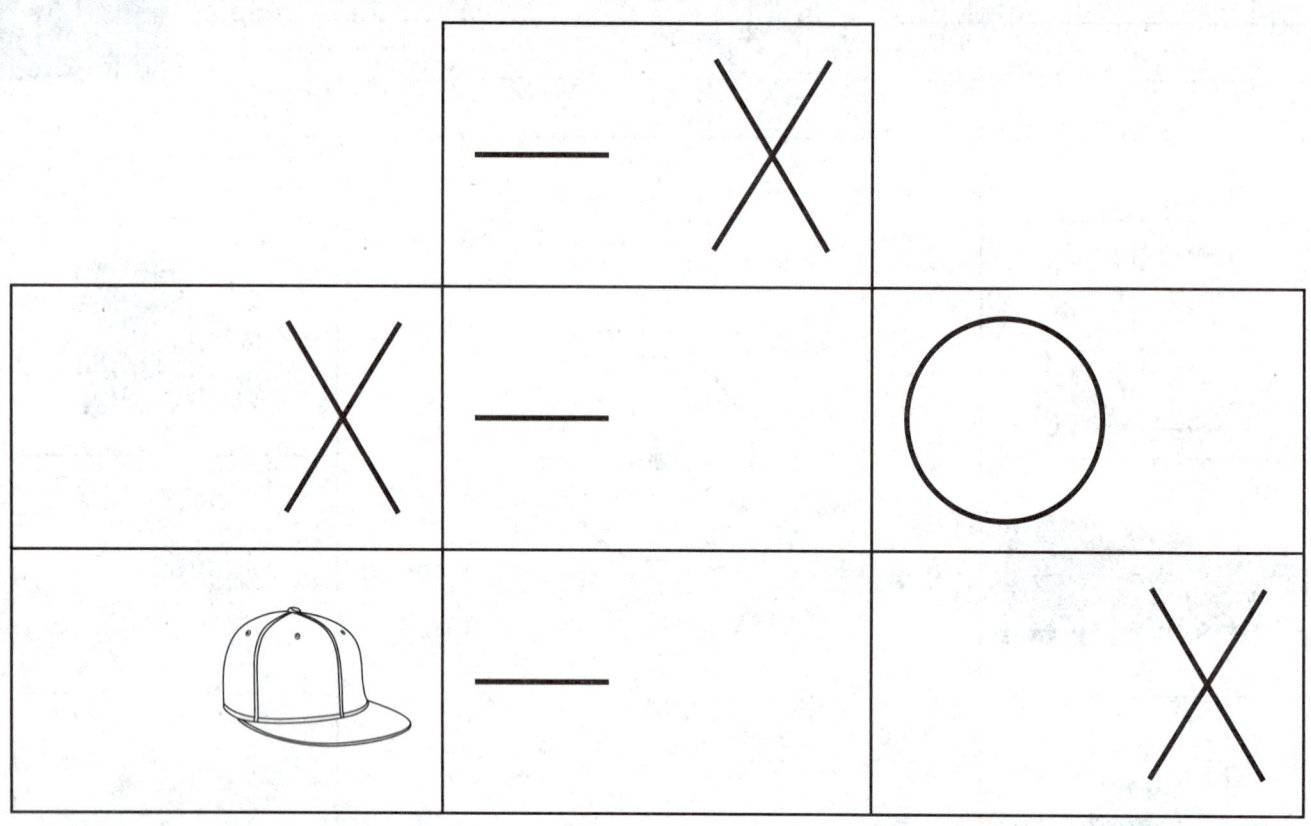

Side 2

_____

_____

1. the dog was old.

2. she is happy.

3. a cat likes to sleep.

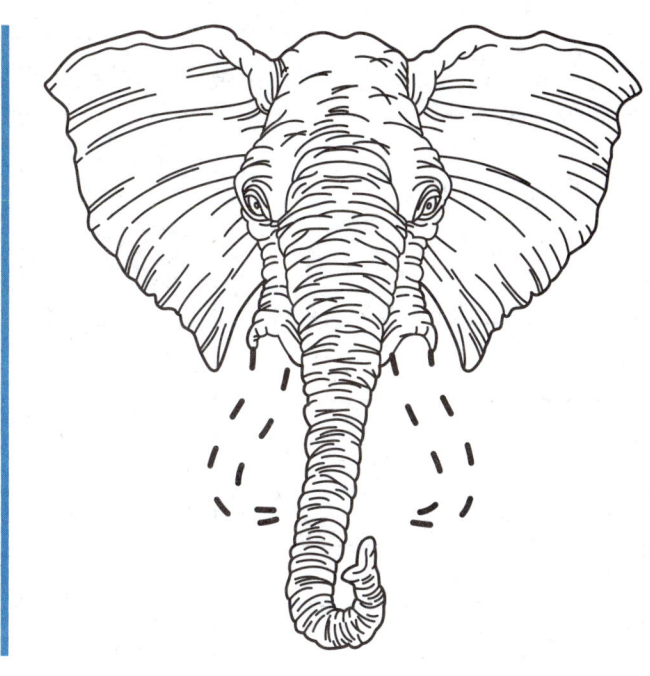

Side 1

Side 2

1. We can fly.

2. the crow had a tail.

3. she likes the kite i made.

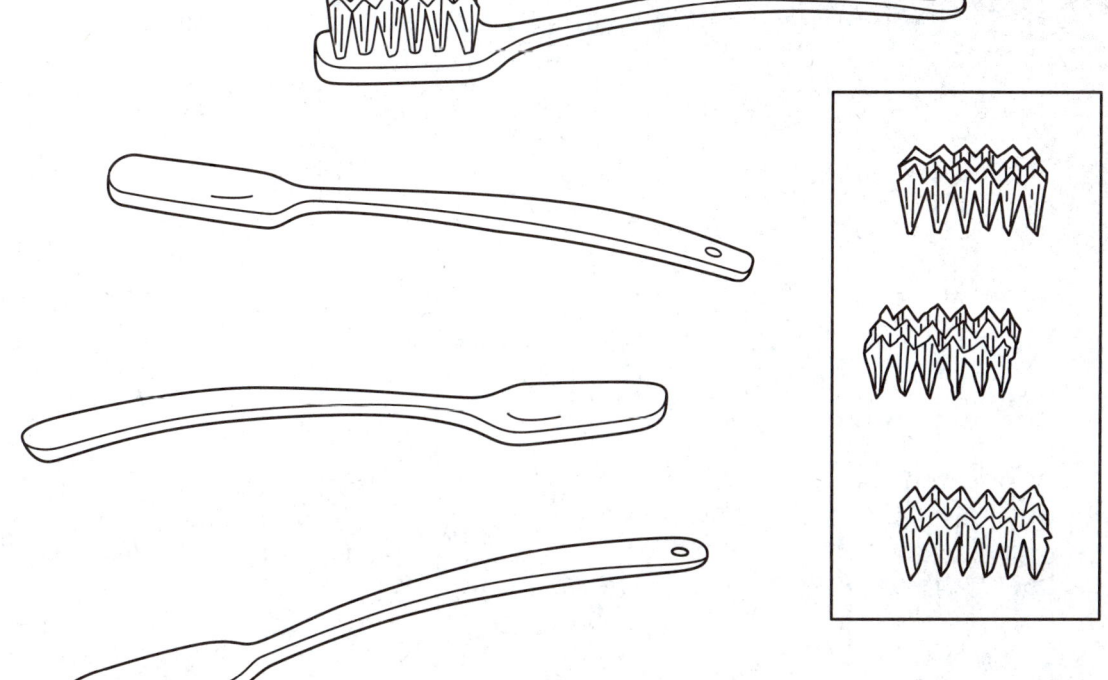

Side 2

_____

1. five cats had fun.

2. Ann and i sat in sand.

3. Can that dog swim?

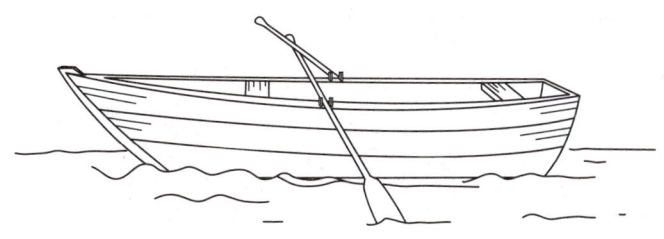

Side 1

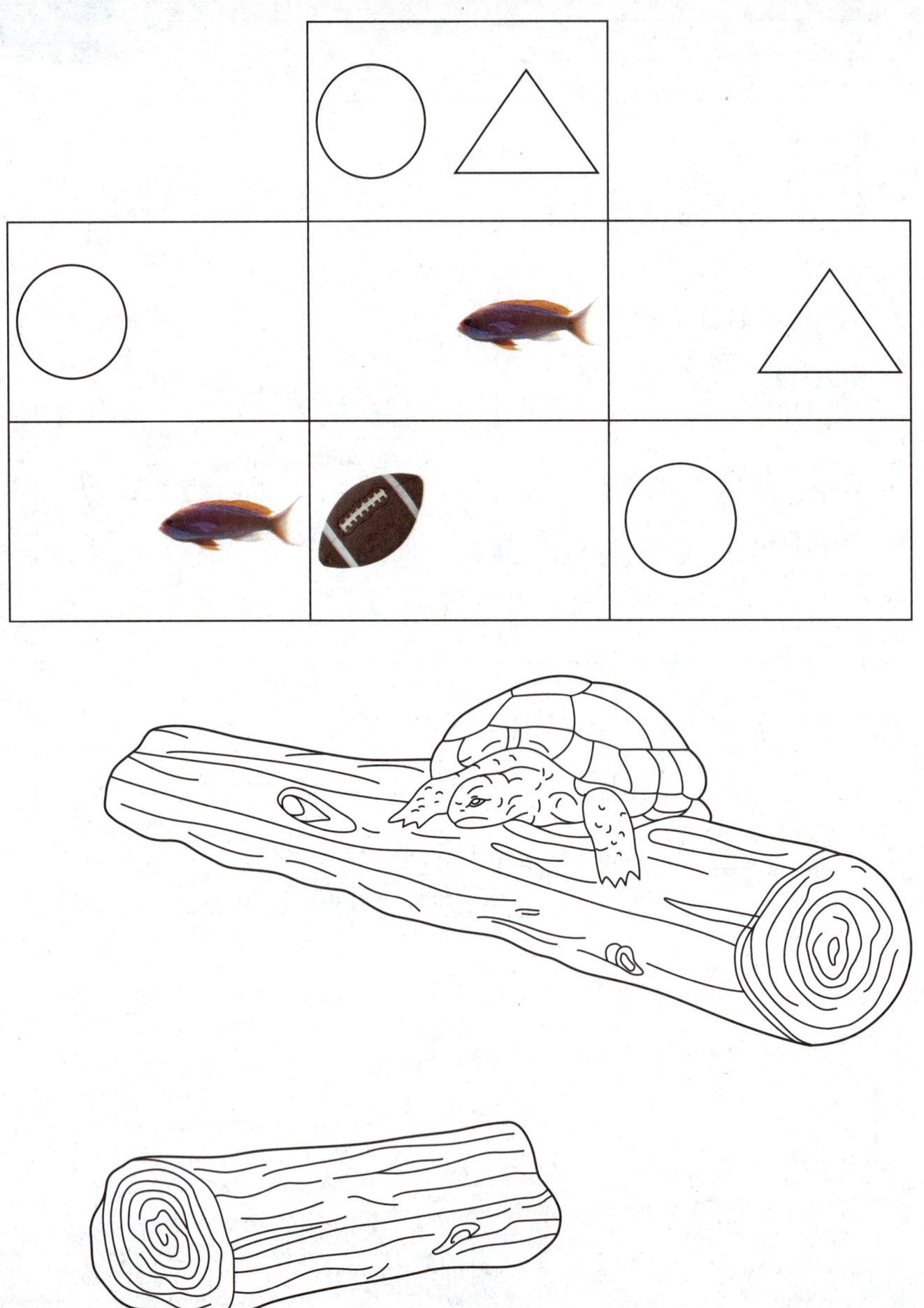

Side 2

1. The bird was in a tree

2. his shirt is brown

3. She and i rode bikes.

Side 1

Side 2

1. pat and i went to the store

2. the book was long.

3. Sam dug a hole

4. my mom plays with a goat

Side 2

PHOTO CREDITS

L006 (car)Henrik5000/Getty Images **L008** (tree)Photographer's Choice/Getty Images (shoe)McGraw-Hill Education (table)McGraw-Hill Education (girl)McGraw-Hill Education/Ken Cavanagh (dog)Purestock/SuperStock (fish)McGraw-Hill Education (chair)Ingram Publishing/SuperStock (book)McGraw-Hill Education **L009** (sandwich)lynx/iconotec.com/Glowimages (cat)G.K. & Vikki Hart/Getty Images (burger)©Ingram Publishing/Alamy (flower)©Alexander Chernyakov/Getty Images (car)Henrik5000/Getty Images (man)Purestock/Getty Images (woman)©Westend61/SuperStock (flag)Getty Images **L010** (tree) Photographer's Choice/Getty Images (cowboy hat)Iconotec/Glow Images (picnic table)lightwise/123RF (bottle)Ingram Publishing/SuperStock (chair)Ingram Publishing/SuperStock (bike)Creative Crop/Getty Images (house)©CreativeCorner/Alamy (clock)Ingram Publishing (book)McGraw-Hill Education **L011** (tree) Photographer's Choice/Getty Images (table)Ingram Publishing/SuperStock (baseball)Richard Hutchings (car) Henrik5000/Getty Images (banana)lynx/iconotec.com/Glow Images (desk)MileA/iStockphoto/Getty Images (pony)anakondasp/iStock/Getty Images (monkey)Sean White/Design Pics/Sean White (shelves)McGraw-Hill Education/Matt Meadows **L012** (dog)Erica Simone Leeds (bus)Martine Oger/123RF (shirt)Ingram Publishing (woman)Comstock/SuperStock (window)GraficallyMinded/Alamy (clock)Greg Nicholas/Getty Images (girl) McGraw-Hill Education/Ken Cavanagh (house)Graeme Pitman (bottle)Getty Images **L013** (boy)rubberball/Getty Images (cup)© McGraw-Hill Education (flag)pbakerp/Getty Images (bike)Creative Crop/Getty Images (door)Chris Rose/Getty Images (cabinet)Ingram Publishing/SuperStock (box)C Squared Studios/Getty Images (glass)Andrey_Kuzmin/Getty Images **L014** (kite)D. Hurst/Alamy (book)McGraw-Hill Education (boy) rubberball/Getty Images (cup)Iconotec/Glow Images (man)Purestock/Getty Images (bus)Martine Oger/123RF (crayon)Charles Brutlag/Getty Images (horse)©Juniors Bildarchiv/Alamy (box)C Squared Studios/Getty Images (glass)Andrey_Kuzmin/Getty Images **L015** (burger)©Ingram Publishing/Alamy (flower)©Alexander Chernyakov/Getty Images (fish)Naturepix/Alamy (cat)© McGraw-Hill Education (monkey)Sean White/Design Pics/Sean White (deer)©Ilene MacDonald/Alamy (wagon)©Comstock Images/Alamy (turtle)© McGraw-Hill Education/Mark Dierker **L016** (cat)G.K. & Vikki Hart/Getty Images (chair) Ingram Publishing/SuperStock (car)Georgii Dolgykh/123RF (bike)©Lawrence Manning/Corbis (shelves) McGraw-Hill Education/Matt Meadows (clock)Greg Nicholas/Getty Images (cabinet)Ingram Publishing/SuperStock (girl)David Buffington/Getty Images **L017** (monkey)Sean White/Design Pics/Sean White (cat) G.K. & Vikki Hart/Getty Images (cowboy hat)Iconotec/Glow Images (bottle)Getty Images (dog)G.K. & Vikki Hart/Getty Images (bus)Martine Oger/123RF (pony)anakondasp/iStock/Getty Images (bike)©Zoonar GmbH/Alamy **L018** (tree)Photographer's Choice/Getty Images (cat)G.K. & Vikki Hart/Getty Images (basset hound) Tetra Images/Alamy (walking cat)Akimasa Harada/Getty Images (dog)©Ingram Publishing/SuperStock (shoe)©D. Hurst/Alamy (rose)©68/Ocean/Corbis (sitting horse)Zuzana Tillerova/123RF (pony)anakondasp/iStock/Getty Images (girl in costume)The McGraw-Hill Companies Inc./Ken Cavanagh Photographer (girl) McGraw-Hill Education/Ken Cavanagh **L019** (boy)Ned Frisk Photography/Corbis (bottle)Ingram Publishing/SuperStock (cup)McGraw-Hill Education (hat)©Comstock Images/Alamy (man)Comstock/SuperStock (woman)Comstock/SuperStock (sitting man)©Image Source, all rights reserved (girl)McGraw-Hill Education/Ken Cavanagh (sitting boy)Ken Cavanagh/McGraw-Hill Education (sitting woman)McGraw-Hill Education (sitting girl)McGraw-Hill Education/Ken Cavanagh **L020** (cat)G.K. & Vikki Hart/Getty Images (horse)©Juniors Bildarchiv/Alamy (man)©Robert Nicholas/age fotostock (sitting man)©Image Source, all rights reserved (sleeping dog)Songphon Kotesopha/123RF (sleeping boy)Blend Images/Getty Images (boy) Ken Cavanagh/McGraw-Hill Education (apple)Author's Image/Glow Images (dog)Dora Zett/Shutterstock.com (sleeping cat)Marcel ter Bekke/Moment/Getty Images **L021** (boy)McGraw-Hill Education/Ken Cavanagh (tree)McGraw-Hill Education (cat)McGraw-Hill Education (horse)©Ingram Publishing/Alamy (baboon)Eric Isselee/Shutterstock.com (sleeping cat)Marcel ter Bekke/Moment/Getty Images (turtle)Jules Frazier/Photodisc/Getty Images (leaf)ventz/Shutterstock.com (sleeping ape)www.galerie-ef.de/Moment/Getty Images (sleeping boy)Ingram Publishing (sleeping horse)Plotitsyna NiNa/Shutterstock.com **L022** (cup) Iconotec/Glow Images (dog)G.K. & Vikki Hart/Getty Images (sleeping man)©Robert Nicholas/age fotostock (horse)©Ingram Publishing/Alamy (sleeping dog)Songphon Kotesopha/123RF (girl)McGraw-Hill Education/Ken Cavanagh (umbrella)Ingram Publishing/SuperStock (sleeping horse)Plotitsyna NiNa/Shutterstock.com (glass)©RelaXimages/Corbis (jar)McGraw-Hill Education (man)McGraw-Hill Education (sleeping girl)©Fancy Collection/SuperStock **L023** (broom)Comstock Images/Getty Images (sleeping cat)©Ingram Publishing/AGE Fotostock (pencil)McGraw-Hill Education/Ken Karp photographer (chair)©Ingram Publishing/Alamy (shelves)McGraw-Hill Education/Matt Meadows (boy)McGraw-Hill Companies Inc./Ken Karp, photographer (cabinet)Ingram Publishing/SuperStock (cat)G.K. & Vikki Hart/Photodisc/Getty Images (woman)Alan Bailey/Rubberball/Getty Images (sleeping cow)AS Food studio/Shutterstock.com (sleeping woman)Robert Nicholas/age fotostock (cow)©Imageshop/Alamy (sleeping boy)Anna Grigorjeva/Shutterstock **L024** (cat) G.K. & Vikki Hart/Getty Images (dog)G.K. & Vikki Hart/Getty Images (red car)Henrik5000/Getty Images (bus) Martine Oger/123RF (blue car)Georgii Dolgykh/123RF (bike)©Lawrence Manning/Corbis (pony)anakondasp/iStock/Getty Images (white car)Paul Piebinga/Getty Images (man)McGraw-Hill Education (boy)McGraw-Hill Education/Ken Cavanagh (girl)iStockphoto/Getty Images (horse)Ingram Publishing (girl eating)BananaStock RF/Getty Images (man eating)© Image Source, all rights reserved. (boy eating)Blend Images/Getty Images **L025** (girl)McGraw-Hill Education/Ken Cavanagh (shoe)©Ingram Publishing/Fotosearch (sleeping cat)©Ingram Publishing/AGE Fotostock (running shoe)©D. Hurst/Alamy (flag)Tetra Images/Getty Images (pony)anakondasp/iStock/Getty Images (horse)©Juniors Bildarchiv/Alamy (shirt)Studiohio (girl eating) BananaStock RF/Getty Images (boy eating)Blend Images/Getty Images (kite)©Tim Hall/cultura/Corbis (cat) Grigorita Ko/Shutterstock.com **L026 Side 01** (clock)Ingram Publishing (9:52 clock)Greg Nicholas/Getty Images (wagon)©Comstock Images/Alamy (colorful leaf)©imagebroker/Alamy (phone)Ingram Publishing/SuperStock (leaf)Image Source/Frazer Cunningham (office phone)©Ingram Publishing/Alamy (smartphone) Gregor Schuster/Getty Images **L026 Side 02** (table)McGraw-Hill Education (cowboy hat)Iconotec/Glow Images (hat)Iconotec/Glow Images (flower)Martin Ruegner/Getty Images (rose)©68/Ocean/Corbis (blue table)Ken Karp/McGraw-Hill Education (deer)©Ilene MacDonald/Alamy (mule deer)Vicki Copeland (cow)©Lex van Lieshout/Imageshop/Alamy (duck)G.K. & Vikki Hart/Photodisc/Getty Images (flapping wings) G.K. & Vikki Hart/Photodisc/Getty Images **L027 Side 01** (tree)Photographer's Choice/Getty Images (shoe) McGraw-Hill Education (cap)Iconotec/Glow Images (banana)McGraw-Hill Education/Mark Dierker, photographer (banana 2)lynx/iconotec.com/Glow Images (car)Georgii Dolgykh/123RF (baboon)Eric Isselee/Shutterstock.com (apple)Stockbyte/Getty Images (egg)Ingram Publishing/SuperStock (ice)©Ingram Publishing/SuperStock (apple/leaf)Lauren Burke/Photographer's Choice RF/Getty Images (sandwich) Carolyn Taylor Photography/Stockbyte/Getty Images (sub sandwich)gbrundin/E+/Getty Images

L027 Side 02 (burger)©Ingram Publishing/Alamy (hamburger)©Ingram Publishing/Alamy (woman)©Westend61/SuperStock (standing woman)Comstock/SuperStock (kite)D. Hurst/Alamy (girl) McGraw-Hill Education/Ken Cavanagh (sitting girl)McGraw-Hill Education/Ken Cavanagh (balloon)©C Squared Studios/Getty Images (kite 2)©Tim Hall/cultura/Corbis (bird)moodboard/Glow Images (blue bird) PanuRuangjan/iStockphoto/Getty Images **L028 Side 01** (tree)Photographer's Choice/Getty Images (ball)© McGraw-Hill Education/Jacques Cornell (car)Henrik5000/Getty Images (deer)©Ilene MacDonald/Alamy (mule deer)Vicki Copeland (black umbrella)Ingram Publishing/SuperStock (iron)Ron Chapple Stock/FotoSearch/Glow Images (umbrella)©Ingram Publishing/Fotosearch (duck)G.K. & Vikki Hart/Photodisc/Getty Images (monkey)Top Photo Engineer/Shutterstock.com (bird)PanuRuangjan/iStockphoto/Getty Images (house)Ryan McVay/Photodisc/Getty Images (flying duck)Antony Grossy/Flickr RF/Getty Images (flying bird)Grant Glendinning Photography/Moment/Getty Images **L028 Side 02** (turtle)© McGraw-Hill Education/Mark Dierker (elephant)McGraw-Hill Education (leaf)ventz/Shutterstock.com (jar)McGraw-Hill Education (colorful leaf)©imagebroker/Alamy (kitchen)©Ingram Publishing/Alamy (phone)©Ingram Publishing/Alamy (white sink)Ingram Publishing/SuperStock (elephant 2)©Ingram Publishing/Alamy (jar w/lid) Steven Frame/Alamy (box turtle)Ingram Publishing/age fotostock (smartphone)Gregor Schuster/Getty Images **L029 Side 01** (dog)Tetra Images/Alamy (cowboy hat)Iconotec/Glow Images (fish)Fuse/Getty Images (flower)©Alexander Chernyakov/Getty Images (yellow flower)Martin Ruegner/Getty Images (tree) Exactostock/Exactostock/SuperStock (bike)Creative Crop/Getty Images (yellow bike)©Lawrence Manning/Corbis (monkey)Sean White/Design Pics/Sean White (elephant)McGraw-Hill Education (cow)©Imageshop/Alamy (elephant 2)©Ingram Publishing/Alamy (black cow)StompingGirl/Shutterstock.com (black/white cow) G.K. & Vikki Hart/Photodisc/Getty Images **L029 Side 02** (cup)McGraw-Hill Education (cat)©Ingram Publishing/AGE Fotostock (tea cup)Iconotec/Glow Images (kitten)Ingram Publishing (glass)Andrey_Kuzmin/Getty Images (wagon)David Buffington/Getty Images (duck)G.K. & Vikki Hart/Photodisc/Getty Images (flying duck)Antony Grossy/Flickr RF/Getty Images (wagon 2)C Squared Studios/Photodisc/Getty Images (glass 2) McGraw-Hill Education (broom)Comstock Images/Getty Images **L030 Side 01** (tree)McGraw-Hill Education (bottle)Ingram Publishing/SuperStock (hat)Iconotec/Glow Images (tree 2)Perfect Picture Parts/Alamy (fish)©Wojtek Kalinowski Photography/Corbis (book)RTimages/Alamy (tree 3)McGraw-Hill Education (glass) Andrey_Kuzmin/Getty Images (leaf)ventz/Shutterstock.com (colorful leaf)©imagebroker/Alamy (green leaf) Image Source/Frazer Cunningham (kite)©Tim Hall/cultura/Corbis (turtle)Ingram Publishing/age fotostock (book 2)McGraw-Hill Education **L030 Side 02** (house)©CreativeCorner/Alamy (5:55 clock)Ingram Publishing (shirt)Ingram Publishing (clock)©Ingram Publishing/Alamy (crayon)Charles Brutlag/Getty Images (shirt)Studiohio (iron)Ron Chapple Stock/FotoSearch/Glow Images (umbrella)Ingram Publishing (house 2) Ryan McVay/Photodisc/Getty Images (red crayon)C Squared Studios/Photodisc/Getty Images **L031 Side 01** (cap)Iconotec/Glow Images (ball)© McGraw-Hill Education/Jacques Cornell (hat)Iconotec/Glow Images (basketball)George Diebold/Getty Images (red balloon)©C Squared Studios/Getty Images (bird)PanuRuangjan/iStockphoto/Getty Images (goat)Svetlana Foote/Alamy (moon)Don Joski/iStockphoto/Getty Images (boat)Randy Lincks/Corbis (coat)©Leonid Nyshko/Alamy (blue balloon)Ingram Publishing/SuperStock (yellow balloon)Ingram Publishing/SuperStock (red bird)Daniel Dempster Photography/Alamy (crayon)Hemera/Getty Images **L031 Side 02** (blue door)Chris Rose/Getty Images (cat) G.K. & Vikki Hart/Getty Images (sleeping cat)©Ingram Publishing/AGE Fotostock (blue window)Richard Goerg/Getty Images (horse)©Ingram Publishing/Alamy (pony)anakondasp/iStock/Getty Images (window) Getty Images/iStockphoto (door)Design Pics/Carson Ganci (tiger)Shutterstock/nattanan726 (giraffe)©Ingram Publishing/Alamy (close giraffe)©Josh Sommers /Getty Images (close tiger)Rene Frederic/Pixtal/AGE Fotostock (ship)©NAN/Alamy Stock Photo **L032 Side 01** (ship docked)©Medioimages/Superstock (cat)Purestock/SuperStock (cowboy hat)Iconotec/Glow Images (car)McGraw-Hill Companies, Inc. Mark Dierker, photographer (school bus)Martine Oger/123RF (bike)Creative Crop/Getty Images (blue car)Georgii Dolgykh/123RF (wagon)©Comstock Images/Alamy (rat)Digital Vision Ltd./SuperStock (doormat) Ingram Publishing/SuperStock (bat)CrackerClips/Getty Images (bus)Doug Sherman/Geofile (black motorcycle)Anatoli Kosolapov/123RF (yellow motorcycle)deusexlupus/123RF (motorcycle)©Oleksiy Maksymenko/Alamy **L032 Side 02** (black/white dog)©Ingram Publishing/SuperStock (dog)Purestock/SuperStock (ice)©Ingram Publishing/SuperStock (ice 2)©Sjoerd van der Wal/Getty Images (phone)©Ingram Publishing/Alamy (hatchet)©Ingram Publishing/AGE Fotostock (axe)©Ingram Publishing/Alamy (polar bear) Dawn Wilson Photography/Getty Images (toothbrush)©McGraw-Hill Education/Ken Karp (smartphone) Gregor Schuster/Getty Images (blue toothbrush)©Ingram Publishing/Alamy (bear)Getty Images/Radius Images **L033 Side 01** (bottle)Ingram Publishing/SuperStock L033 Side 01 (shirt)Ingram Publishing (elephant)McGraw-Hill Education (duck)G.K. & Vikki Hart/Photodisc/Getty Images (walking giraffe)Chris Clor/Blend Images (giraffe)©Ingram Publishing/Alamy (tiger)Rene Frederic/Pixtal/AGE Fotostock (bear)©Life on white/Alamy Stock Photo (flag)©Comstock Images/Alamy (rag)Sergei Vinogradov/123RF (bear 2)Getty Images/Radius Images **L033 Side 02** (docked ship)©Medioimages/Superstock (blue fish) Fuse/Getty Images (fish)Andrew Ilyasov/Getty Images (kite)D. Hurst/Alamy (sink)©Ingram Publishing/Alamy (kite 2)©Tim Hall/cultura/Corbis (bird)PanuRuangjan/iStockphoto/Getty Images (white sink)Comstock Images/Getty Images (red bird)Daniel Dempster Photography/Alamy (tiger)Shutterstock/nattanan726 (stove)INSADCO Photography/Alamy (ship)©EvrenKalinbacak/Getty Image (stove 2)Arina Zaiachin/123RF **L034 Side 01** (cat)Purestock/SuperStock (ball)© McGraw-Hill Education/Jacques Cornell (iron)Ron Chapple Stock/FotoSearch/Glow Images (phone)Ingram Publishing/SuperStock (balloon)©C Squared Studios/Getty Images (office phone)©Ingram Publishing/Alamy (hatchet)©Ingram Publishing/Alamy (axe)©McGraw-Hill Education/Ken Karp (toothbrush)©McGraw-Hill Education/Ken Karp (smartphone) Gregor Schuster/Getty Images (blue toothbrush)©Ingram Publishing/Alamy (baseball)Photodisc/Getty Images (rat)Ilia Shcherbakov/123RF (axe 2)Siede Preis/Getty Images (oar)McGraw-Hill Education **L034 Side 02** (chair)Ingram Publishing/SuperStock (wood/metal chair)Ingram Publishing/SuperStock (man) Purestock/Getty Images (woman)©Westend61/SuperStock (photographer)Comstock/SuperStock (standing woman)Comstock/SuperStock (cow)©Imageshop/Alamy (balloon)Ingram Publishing/SuperStock (couch) Iuliia Nazarenko/123RF (sofa)Pix11/Shutterstock.com (black/white cow)G.K. & Vikki Hart/Getty Images **L035 Side 01** (bottle)Getty Images (cup)McGraw-Hill Education (glass)Andrey_Kuzmin/Getty Images (ice)©Ingram Publishing/SuperStock (glass 2)©RelaXimages/Corbis (sink)©Ingram Publishing/Alamy (white sink)Comstock Images/Getty Images (stove)INSADCO Photography/Alamy (stove 2)Arina Zaiachin/123RF (rug)©Ingram Publishing/Fototsearch (snake)Shutterstock/cynoclub (cake)©JupiterMedia/Alamy **L035 Side 02** (car)Henrik5000/Getty Images (bike)Creative Crop/Getty Images (yellow bike)©Lawrence

Manning/Corbis (white car)Paul Piebinga/Getty Images (duck)G.K. & Vikki Hart/Photodisc/Getty Images (mallard)PaulTessier/E+/Getty Images (standing tiger)Shutterstock/nattanan726 (walking giraffe)Chris Clor/Blend Images (giraffe)©Josh Sommers /Getty Images (yellow motorcycle)deusexlupus/123RF (motorcycle)©Oleksiy Maksymenko/Alamy (tiger)McGraw-Hill Education/Cleveland Metroparks Zoo (ladybug)Fotosearch/Getty Images **L036 Side 01** (blue shoe)McGraw-Hill Education (cowboy hat)Iconotec/Glow Images (shoe)Ingram Publishing/SuperStock (girl)McGraw-Hill Education/Ken Cavanagh (cap)Iconotec/Glow Images (hat)Iconotec/Glow Images (dog)Purestock/SuperStock (boy)McGraw-Hill Education/Ken Cavanagh (clock)Ingram Publishing (shirt)Ingram Publishing (red shirt)Studiohio (boat)Darryl Brooks/Shutterstock.com (goat)Dmitri Gomon/Shutterstock.com (jeans)C Squared Studios/Photodisc/Getty Images (toy)Burke Triolo Productions/Brand X Pictures/PunchStock **L036 Side 02** (tree)Photographer's Choice/Getty Images (tree 2)McGraw-Hill Education (ball)The McGraw-Hill Companies, Inc./Jacques Cornell photographer (book)RTimages/Alamy (pencil)McGraw-Hill Education/Ken Karp photographer (basketball)George Diebold/Getty Images (U.S. flag)Getty Images (school bus)Martine Oger/123RF (bus)Doug Sherman/Geofile (flag)creisinger/Getty Images (blue pencil)Potapova Valeriya/Hemera/Getty Images (book)Dot Box Inc./McGraw-Hill Education **L037 Side 01** (car)Drazen Vukelic/Getty Images (bird)Grant Glendinning Photography/Moment/Getty Images (bear)Christina Krutz/Radius Images/Getty Images **L037 Side 02** (hat)Iconotec/Glow Images (broom)Comstock Images/Getty Images (cat)©Ingram Publishing/AGE Fotostock (sandwich)Ingram Publishing/age fotostock.com/Glowimages (monkey eating)Sean White/Design Pics/Sean White (horse)©Juniors Bildarchiv/Alamy (monkey)©Ingram Publishing/Alamy (house)Graeme Pitman (deer)©Ilene MacDonald/Alamy (broken egg)Ingram Publishing (apple)Author's Image/Glow Images (umbrella)Ingram Publishing (shelves)Thinkstock/Getty Images (cow)©Imageshop/Alamy (yellow house)Ryan McVay/Photodisc/Getty Images (black cow)Stompingbilly/Dreamstime.com (egg)Siede Preis/Photodisc/Getty Images (bookcase)luchschen/123RF (sandwich)gbrundin/E+/Getty Images (deer running)Tom Reichner/Shutterstock **L038 Side 01** (chair)Ingram Publishing/SuperStock (bear)Getty Images/Radius Images (rabbit)Rubberball/Getty Images **L038 Side 02** (ball)The McGraw-Hill Education/Jacques Cornell photographer (pencil)McGraw-Hill Education/Ken Karp photographer (basketball)George Diebold/Getty Images (sailboat)Randy Lincks/Corbis (wooden bat)CrackerClips/Getty Images (bat)Photodisc/Getty Images (oars)McGraw-Hill Education (pencil eraser)Ryan McVay/Photodisc/Getty Images (pencil)Jacques Cornell/McGraw-Hill Education (eraser)Ryan McVay/Photodisc/Getty Images (paddles)©Ingram Publishing/Alamy (boat)Comstock Images/Alamy **L039 Side 01** (ball) © McGraw-Hill Education/Jacques Cornell (fish)Ammit/Getty Images (blue window)Richard Goerg/Getty Images (blue door)Chris Rose/Getty Images (car)Georgii Dolgykh/123RF (wooden window)Getty Images (turtle)© McGraw-Hill Education/Mark Dierker (window)Ingram Publishing/SuperStock (door)Design Pics/Carson Ganci (box turtle)Ingram Publishing/age fotostock (ship)Ingram Publishing (truck)Andrey Pavlov/Shutterstock **L039 Side 02** (tree)Perfect Picture Parts/Alamy (tree 2)Exactostock/Exactostock/SuperStock (glass)Andrey_Kuzmin/Getty Images (elephant)McGraw-Hill Education (ice)©Ingram Publishing/SuperStock (ice 2)Sjoerd van der Wal/Getty Images (leaf)ventz/Shutterstock.com (glass 2)RelaXimages/Corbis (oak leaf)Image Source/Frazer Cunningham (elephant 2)Shutterstock/sevenke (brown goat)Dmitri Gomon/Shutterstock.com (goat)Getty Images/iStockphoto **L040 Side 01** (fish)McGraw-Hill Education (moon)Don Joski/iStockphoto/Getty Images **L040 Side 02** (banana)lynx/iconotec/Glow Images (rose)©68/Ocean/Corbis (desk)MileA/iStockphoto/Getty Images (cabinet)Ingram Publishing/SuperStock (sink)Ingram Publishing/SuperStock (blue/white iron)Floortje/Getty Images (brown desk)Svetlana Happyland/Shutterstock.com (office desk)Artbox/Shutterstock.com (iron)Ron Chapple Stock/FotoSearch/Glow Images **L041 Side 01** (keys)Creatas/Punchstock (fish)©Wojtek Kalinowski Photography/Corbis (book)RTimages/Alamy (dog)G.K. & Vikki Hart/Getty Images (bat)Photodisc/Getty Images (rat)Ilia Shcherbakov/123RF (goat)Dmitri Gomon/Shutterstock.com (doormat)McGraw-Hill Education (pig)svetlana foote/123RF (balloon)C Squared Studios/Photodisc/Getty Images **L042 Side 01** (car)Drazen Vukelic/Getty Images (bus)Doug Sherman/Geofile (flag)Comstock Images/Alamy (bird)ronniechua/123RF (motorcycle)gors4730/123RF **L042 Side 02** (dog)Sharon Montrose/Getty Images (pig)yevgeniy11/Shutterstock.com (frog)Digital Vision/PunchStock (log)Lev Kropotov/Shutterstock **L043 Side 01** (horse)©Ingram Publishing/Alamy (bike)©Lawrence Manning/Corbis (kite)D. Hurst/Alamy (bear)Christina Krutz/Radius Images/Getty Images (tiger)Shutterstock/nattanan726 (head)Getty Images/Fuse (bed)Judith Collins/Alamy Stock Photo (sled)Ingram Publishing/SuperStock (deer)denise coyle/123RF **L043 Side 02** (window)Richard Goerg/Getty Images (car)©Drazen Vukelic/Getty Images **L044 Side 01** (cat)©Ingram Publishing/AGE Fotostock (horse)©Ingram Publishing/Alamy (cow)Diajal/Shutterstock.com (boy)jaroon/iStock/Getty Images Plus/Getty Images (man)McGraw-Hill Education **L044 Side 02** (cat)G.K. & Vikki Hart/Getty Images (man)Purestock/Getty Images (woman)©Westend61/SuperStock (hat)©Thinkstock/Alamy (can)Jeffrey Coolidge/Photodisc/Getty Images (fan)McGraw-Hill Education **L045 Side 01** (dog)G.K. & Vikki Hart/Getty Images (cat)McGraw-Hill Education (pony)anakondasp/iStock/Getty Images **L045 Side 02** (hat)Iconotec/Glow Images (goat)Svetlana Foote/Alamy (coat)©Leonid Nyshko/Alamy (boat)Darryl Brooks/Shutterstock.com **L046 Side 01** (car)McGraw-Hill Companies, Inc. Mark Dierker, photographer (tree)©Lars A. Niki (pencil)Potapova Valeriya/Hemera/Getty Images **L046 Side 02** (man)Comstock/SuperStock (cow)©Imageshop/Alamy (rabbit)Rubberball/Getty Images (pig)yevgeniy11/Shutterstock.com (bat)cheri131/Getty Images (sandbox)imagebroker/Alamy (hand)Thawat Tanhai/123RF (rubber band)© McGraw-Hill Education/Ken Cavanagh (owl)Corbis Super RF/Alamy (white rabbit)StockPhotosArt/Shutterstock (waste basket)©McGraw-Hill Education/Ken Karp (rabbit standing)Getty Images/Vetta (owl/flowers)Shutterstock/Dagmara Ksandrova **L047 Side 01** (table)Ingram Publishing/SuperStock (clock)Ingram Publishing (bike)Fuse/Getty Images (wagon)David Buffington/Getty Images (sink)Ingram Publishing/Alamy (bus)dra_schwartz/E+/Getty Images **L047 Side 02** (flower)Martin Ruegner/Getty Images (rose)©68/Ocean/Corbis (glass)©RelaXimages/Corbis (colorful leaf)©imagebroker/Alamy (leaf)Image Source (bed)Judith Collins/Alamy Stock Photo (can)Jeffrey Coolidge/Photodisc/Getty Images (bowl)eskaylim/iStockphoto/Getty Images (cola can)Kutay Tanir/Getty Images **L048 Side 01** (wooden bat)CrackerClips/Getty Images (bat)cheri131/Getty Images (dog)Calamorlanda/Flickr/Getty Images (tree bark)Aaron Roeth Photography (saw)McGraw-Hill Education/Mark Steinmetz (girl)Blend Images/Alamy (playground)Shutterstock/zstock (river)Pixtal/age fotostock (bank)fasthorses/Shutterstock.com (snowy road)Miha9000/iStock/Getty Images Plus/Getty Images **L048 Side 02** (cat)Akimasa Harada/Getty Images (cake)©Stockbyte/PunchStock (bird)bookguy/iStockphoto/Getty Images **L049 Side 01** (man)©4x6/Getty Images (wave)Shutterstock/EpicStockMedia (coast)keleny/123RF (woman)Beth Van Trees/123RF (playground)Shutterstock/zstock (river)Pixtal/age fotostock (bank)fasthorses/Shutterstock.com (snowy road)Miha9000/iStock/Getty Images Plus/Getty Images (airplane)Ingram Publishing/SuperStock (boy)Kent Hilbert/Alamy Stock Photo **L050 Side 01** (baseball bat)Photodisc/Getty Images (bat)cheri131/Getty Images (tree bark)Aaron Roeth Photography (bank)fasthorses/Shutterstock.com (saw)Ingram Publishing/SuperStock (boy)Kent Hilbert/Alamy Stock Photo (dog)Calamorlanda/Flickr/Getty Images (saw)Jupiterimages/Getty Images (girl)Blend Images/Alamy **L050 Side 02** (fish)Karen Gowlett-Holmes/Getty Images (can)Photodisc **L051 Side 01** (ball)McGraw-Hill Education/Jacques Cornell (broken egg)Ingram Publishing/SuperStock (hatchet)©Ingram Publishing/AGE Fotostock (axe)Siede Preis/Getty Images (ear)Voronin76/Shutterstock (egg)Siede Preis/Getty Images (dog ears)Purestock/Getty Images **L051 Side 02** (cake)©Stockbyte/PunchStock (snake)G.K. & Vikki Hart/Getty Images (bird)Mmphotos/Getty Images (dog)©McGraw-Hill Education **L052 Side 01** (basset hound)Tetra Images/Alamy (bottle)Getty Images (hamburger)©Ingram Publishing/Alamy (burger)McGraw-Hill Education (fish)Naturepix/Alamy (U.S. flag)Tetra Images/Getty Images (cat)Ingram Publishing/SuperStock (horse)©Juniors Bildarchiv/Alamy (dog)Erica Simone Leeds (turtle)Jules Frazier/Photodisc/Getty Images (kite)©Tim Hall/cultura/Corbis (flag)creisinger/Getty Images (bird)Grant Glendinning Photography/Moment/Getty Images **L053 Side 01** (cat)Akimasa Harada/Getty Images (bird)Richard Hutchings (dog)G.K. & Vikki Hart/Getty Images (wagon)David Buffington/Getty Images (hat)Iconotec/Glow Images (hat w/flowers)©Comstock Images/Alamy (wagon 2)C Squared Studios/Photodisc/Getty Images (balloon)Ingram Publishing/SuperStock (wooden bat)CrackerClips/Getty Images **L054 Side 01** (pencil)McGraw-Hill Education/Jacques Cornell photographer (cup)Iconotec/Glow Images (banana)lynx/ iconotec/Glow Images (banana 2)McGraw-Hill Education/Mark Dierker, photographer (tree)McGraw-Hill Education (car)McGraw-Hill Companies, Inc. Mark Dierker, photographer (bike)Creative Crop/Getty Images (dog)Erica Simone Leeds (wagon)©Comstock Images/Alamy (silver bike)©Getty Images GmbH/Alamy (ice)©Ingram Publishing/SuperStock (ice 2)©Sjoerd van der Wal/Getty Images (log)Lev Kropotov/Shutterstock **L055 Side 02** (shoe)Ingram Publishing/SuperStock (grey shoe)©Ingram Publishing/Fotosearch (fish)Karen Gowlett-Holmes/Getty Images (pink fish)McGraw-Hill Education/Dallas World Aquarium (dog)Songphon Kotesopha/123RF (sliced apple)Stockbyte/Getty Images (apple)McGraw-Hill Education (bird)Daniel Dempster Photography/Alamy (axe)Siede Preis/Getty Images (snake)Shutterstock/cynoclub (cake)Comstock Images/Alamy **L056 Side 02** (table)McGraw-Hill Education (broom)Comstock Images/Getty Images (car)McGraw-Hill Education/Ken Karp photographer (car)Henrik5000/Getty Images (round table)Dejan Jekic/123RF (car 2)McGraw-Hill Companies, Inc. Mark Dierker, photographer (classic car)©Drazen Vukelic/Getty Images (boy)Ken Cavanagh/McGraw-Hill Education (tree)©Lars A. Niki (door)Design Pics/Carson Ganci (apple)Lauren Burke/Photographer's Choice RF/Getty Images (star)Malosee Dolo/123RF (sitting boy)McGraw-Hill Education (moon)©Eyebyte/Alamy **L057 Side 01** (moon)©Eyebyte/Alamy **L057 Side 02** (cup)McGraw-Hill Education (car)Henrik5000/Getty Images (shoe)©D. Hurst/Alamy (house)©CreativeCorner/Alamy **L058 Side 01** (classic car)Paul Piebinga/Getty Images (bus)Doug Sherman/Geofile (boat)Comstock Images/Alamy (truck)Getty Images/iStockphoto/Shutterstock (train)©Image Source Plus/Alamy Stock Photo (canoe) © Comstock Images/Alamy (car) © McGraw-Hill Education (taxi)Stockdisc/Getty Images (taxi 2)Stockbyte/Punchstock **L058 Side 02** (house)©CreativeCorner/Alamy (sliced apple)Stockbyte/Getty Images (apple)Author's Image/Glow Images (tree)©Lars A. Niki (door)Design Pics/Carson Ganci (apple)©JupiterMedia/Alamy (moon)Potapova Valeriya/Hemera/Getty Images (moon)©Eyebyte/Alamy (orange)lynx/ iconotec/Glow Images (eye)Anthony Lee /Getty Images (eye side)Glowimages/Getty Images (sliced orange)McGraw-Hill Education/Mark Steinmetz (carrot)©Clover/Getty Images **L059 Side 02** (shoe)©Ingram Publishing/Fotosearch (broom)Comstock Images/Getty Images (bike)©Zoonar GmbH/Alamy (star)Malosee Dolo/123RF (moon)©Eyebyte/Alamy (cat)G.K. & Vikki Hart/Getty Images **L060 Side 02** (shoe)Ingram Publishing/SuperStock (car)Georgii Dolgykh/123RF (cake)©Stockbyte/PunchStock (moon) ©Eyebyte/Alamy (hat)Iconotec/Glow Images **L061 Side 02** (shoe)C. Zachariasen/PhotoAlto (bike)©Zoonar GmbH/Alamy (cake)©JupiterMedia/Alamy (star)Malosee Dolo/123RF (moon)©Eyebyte/Alamy (spoon)Kim DeClaire/Getty Image **L062 Side 01** (shoe)McGraw-Hill Education (table)Ingram Publishing/SuperStock (ball)The McGraw-Hill Companies, Inc./Jacques Cornell photographer (hat)Iconotec/Glow Images (BMX bike)Creative Crop/Getty Images (car)Paul Piebinga/Getty Images (bike)Fuse/Getty Images (boat)Comstock Images/Alamy (apple)Lauren Burke/Photographer's Choice RF/Getty Images **L062 Side 02** (flower)Martin Ruegner/Getty Images (chair)Ingram Publishing/SuperStock (bike)Creative Crop/Getty Images (kite)D. Hurst/Alamy (door)Design Pics/Carson Ganci (house)Ryan McVay/Photodisc/Getty Images **L063 Side 01** (motorcycle)gors4730/123RF (rose)©68/Ocean/Corbis (car)Georgii Dolgykh/123RF (flag)©Comstock Images/Alamy (basket)McGraw-Hill Education/Mark Steinmetz (banana)Burke Triolo Productions/Artville/Getty Images (airplane)ansonsaw/E+/Getty Images (bin)©Ingram Publishing/Alamy **L063 Side 02** (dog)Tetra Images/Alamy (cat)Akimasa Harada/Getty Images (bottle)Getty Images (baseball)Richard Hutchings (moon)Don Joski/iStockphoto/Getty Images (sock)Ken Cavanagh/McGraw-Hill Education **L064 Side 01** (cat)G.K. & Vikki Hart/Getty Images (ball)The McGraw-Hill Companies, Inc./Jacques Cornell photographer (car)McGraw-Hill Education/Mark Dierker, photographer (truck)Getty Images (house)©CreativeCorner/Alamy (turtle)McGraw-Hill Education/Mark Dierker, photographer (balloon)©C Squared Studios/Getty Images (boat)Comstock Images/Alamy (truck)Getty Images/iStockphoto/Sharon Meredith **L064 Side 02** (car)Henrik5000/Getty Images (tree)McGraw-Hill Education (glass)Andrey_Kuzmin/Getty Images (leaf)Image Source/Frazer Cunningham (bee)Tomasz Pietryszek/E+/Getty Images **L067 Side 02** (cap)Iconotec/Glow Images (hat)Iconotec/Glow Images (pencil)McGraw-Hill Education/Ken Karp photographer (flower)Martin Ruegner/Getty Images (tree)©Lars A. Niki (scissors)Siede Preis/Getty Images (cat)Shutterstock/Steve Heap **L068 Side 01** (cap)Iconotec/Glow Images (bus)The McGraw-Hill Companies, Inc./Ken Karp photographer (car)Henrik5000/Getty Images **L069 Side 01** (car)Georgii Dolgykh/123RF (box)C Squared Studios/Getty Images (cow)©Imageshop/Alamy (turtle)Ingram Publishing/age fotostock (book)McGraw-Hill Education (saw)Randy Lincks/Corbis (airplane)Bim/Getty Images (bus)Fuse/Getty Images **L070 Side 01** (girl)Tetra Images/Alamy (truck)Getty Images/iStockphoto/Sharon Meredith (canoe) © Comstock Images/Alamy (hammer)©Comstock Images/Alamy (cat)Shutterstock/Steve Heap (boat)Ingram Publishing (airplane)Michal Krakowiak/Getty Images (basket)Shutterstock/Serg64 **L072 Side 01** (pencil)McGraw-Hill Education/Ken Karp photographer (shirt)Studiohio (jeans)C Squared Studios/Photodisc/Getty Images (cup)McGraw-Hill Education/Mark Steinmetz (toothbrush)Shevchuk Boris/iStockphoto/Getty Images (book)McGraw-Hill Education/Dot Box Inc. (sock)©McGraw-Hill Education/Ken Cavanagh (doll)©McGraw-Hill Education/Ken Cavanagh **L072 Side 02** (flower) Alexander Chernyakov/Getty Images (banana)lynx/ iconotec.com/Glow Images (car)©Drazen Vukelic/Getty Images (boat)Randy Lincks/Corbis (motorcycle)gors4730/123RF (airplane)Ingram Publishing/SuperStock (basket)McGraw-Hill Education/Mark Steinmetz (bin)©Ingram Publishing/Alamy (flag)Shutterstock/Gts **L073 Side 01** (rose)©68/Ocean/Corbis (table)Dejan Jekic/123RF (window)Getty Images/iStockphoto (book)McGraw-Hill Education (desk)Svetlana Happyland/Shutterstock.com (chair)Ingram Publishing (jar)©Markus Guhl/Getty Images (plate) © McGraw-Hill Education **L073 Side 02** (cat)Purestock/SuperStock (ball)McGraw-Hill Education/Jacques Cornell photographer (car)McGraw-Hill Education/Mark Dierker, photographer (bike)©Zoonar GmbH/Alamy (turtle)Ingram Publishing/age fotostock (balloon)Ingram Publishing/SuperStock (boat)Darryl Brooks/Shutterstock.com (truck)Andrey Pavlov/Shutterstock **L074 Side 01** (table)McGraw-Hill Education (chair)Ingram Publishing/SuperStock (glass)Andrey_Kuzmin/Getty Images (cabinet)Ingram Publishing/SuperStock (book)McGraw-Hill Education (coat)©Leonid Nyshko/Alamy (pencil)tobkatrina/123RF (newspaper)Brand X Pictures/Stockbyte/Getty Images/McGraw-Hill Companies, Inc. Mark Dierker, photographer **L075 Side 01** (bus)Martine Oger/123RF (apple)Author's Image/Glow Images (cake)©JupiterMedia/Alamy (boat)Darryl Brooks/Shutterstock.com (truck)Andrey Pavlov/Shutterstock (bread)Alex Cao/Getty Images (carrot)©Clover/SuperStock **L076 Side 01** (fish)ansonsaw/E+/Getty Images (cup)McGraw-Hill Education/Dot Box Inc. (banana)©McGraw-Hill Education/Mark Dierker (bike)©Zoonar GmbH/Alamy (apple)Lauren Burke/Photographer's Choice RF/Getty Images (coat)©Leonid Nyshko/Alamy (truck)Andrey Pavlov/Shutterstock (cake)©Stockbyte/PunchStock (cheese)Photographer's Choice/Getty Images (boat)Comstock Images/Alamy **L077 Side 02** (cup)Iconotec/Glow Images (Moon)Don Joski/iStockphoto/Getty Images (flag)creisinger/Getty Images (star)Malosee Dolo/123RF **L078 Side 02** (fish)McGraw-Hill Education (football)Photodisc/Getty Images